VEGETARIAN

OVER 100 EASY-TO-FOLLOW RECIPES • EACH RECIPE PHOTOGRAPHED

VEGETARIAN

OVER 100 EASY-TO-FOLLOW RECIPES • EACH RECIPE PHOTOGRAPHED

WELDON
OWEN

Published by Weldon Owen Pty Ltd
59–61 Victoria Street, McMahons Point
Sydney, NSW 2060, Australia
Copyright © 2011 Weldon Owen Pty Ltd

Managing Director Kay Scarlett
Publisher Corinne Roberts
Creative Director Sue Burk
Images Manager Trucie Henderson
Senior Vice President, International Sales Stuart Laurence
Sales Manager, North America Ellen Towell
Administration Manager, International Sales Kristine Ravn
Production Director Todd Rechner
Production and Prepress Controller Mike Crowton
Production Controller Lisa Conway
Production Coordinator Nathan Grice

Designer Chris Andrew
Editorial Director Laura Thomson
Editor Laurie Black
Editorial Assistant Natalie Ryan

Printed by 1010 Printing
Manufactured in China

The paper used in the manufacture of this book is sourced
from wood grown in sustainable forests. It complies with the
Environmental Management System Standard ISO 14001:2004

A WELDON OWEN PRODUCTION

CONTENTS

VEGETARIAN

Welcome to the exciting world of vegetarian cookery, a cuisine that captures nature's bounty and makes the most of what each season brings to the table. In this book, you will discover that great vegetarian food can appeal to everyone .

Vegetarian cooking can be rich and generous, or light and refreshing. The following pages are packed with recipes from all over the world. There are dishes for every day and for special occasions. You will master the classics and enjoy some modern ideas, too.

Inspiration for vegetarian cookery should never be a problem again. Whether you are new to vegetarian cookery, don't know what to serve your vegetarian guests, or just want new and inspiring ways to include more vegetables in your diet, this book is for you. Enjoy the pleasures of a balanced diet!

DIPS &
SNACKS

HOW TO MAKE PESTO

Pesto, one of Italy's most famous sauces, is a breeze to make. Its classic match is pasta, but the delicious basil and pine nut flavor works well in many other recipes, such as omelets and tomato dishes.

Makes 1 cup

¼ cup (30g) pine nuts

4 cups (120g) loosely packed basil leaves

2 cloves garlic, roughly chopped

½ cup (45g) grated parmesan

¼ cup (60ml) extra virgin olive oil

salt

olive oil, for storage

Preheat oven to 350°F (180°C).

STEP 1 Spread the pine nuts evenly in a baking pan. Bake for 5 to 10 minutes, until just starting to color. Leave to cool.

STEP 2 Wash basil leaves and dry thoroughly, using a salad spinner, if you have one, or in a colander, then finish drying on paper towels. Place pine nuts in a food processor along with basil, garlic and parmesan. Pulse on and off to chop the basil.

STEP 3 With motor running slowly, gradually add extra virgin olive oil until the mixture is combined but not quite smooth. Season to taste with salt.

STEP 4 Spoon pesto into a jar and cover surface with a small amount of olive oil to prevent oxidation. Cover jar and refrigerate.

ARTICHOKE PÂTÉ

Serves 6

2 x 12oz (340g) jars
marinated artichoke hearts,
drained

1 cup (60g) fresh
breadcrumbs

3 Tbsp chopped parsley

2 cloves garlic, crushed

3 Tbsp extra virgin olive oil

1 sourdough baguette,
thinly sliced and toasted,
for serving

In a food processor, blend drained artichokes, breadcrumbs, parsley and garlic.

Gradually add olive oil, in a slow steady stream, processing until smooth. Season to taste.

Spoon pâté into a bowl and serve with toast.

SPICY CARROT DIP

Serves 4

1 ½ lb (750g) carrots, peeled and each cut in 4

2 cloves garlic, peeled

¼ cup (60ml) extra virgin olive oil

3 Tbsp red wine vinegar

1 tsp paprika

¼ tsp chili powder

1 tsp ground cumin

1 tsp ground coriander

cilantro (coriander) and mint sprigs, for serving

flat bread, for serving

Place carrots and garlic in a saucepan and cover with salted water. Bring to a boil and cook for 10 minutes, until tender. Drain well.

Mash carrot and garlic roughly and stir in remaining ingredients. Season to taste.

Top with cilantro and mint sprigs and serve with flat bread.

POTATO & GARLIC DIP

Serves 8

12oz (330g) Russet potatoes (or other floury potatoes), peeled

½ cup (125ml) readymade mayonnaise

1 clove garlic, crushed

juice of ½ lemon

vegetables such as beans, carrots or baby beets, for serving

Cook potatoes in a saucepan of boiling salted water until tender. Drain and mash well, or pass through a ricer. Set aside to cool completely.

Place mashed potato in a bowl. Add mayonnaise and garlic and mix well. Stir in lemon juice and season to taste.

Spoon dip into a bowl and serve with vegetables.

SPINACH CREAM CHEESE DIP

Serves 6

7oz (200g) frozen chopped spinach, defrosted

8oz (250g) cream cheese, at room temperature

2 cloves garlic, crushed

1 Tbsp lemon juice

¼ tsp chili powder

¼ tsp ground nutmeg

salt and freshly ground black pepper

sliced crusty bread, for serving

Pat dry defrosted spinach on paper towels to remove as much moisture as possible.

Blend cream cheese, garlic and lemon juice in a food processor until smooth and creamy. Add the spinach and process just to combine.

Add chili powder and nutmeg, and season with salt and pepper, to taste.

Spoon dip into a bowl and serve with crusty bread.

HUMMUS

Serves 6

14oz (400g) can chickpeas, rinsed and drained

3 cloves garlic

1 Tbsp tahini (see glossary, page 306)

juice of 1 to 2 lemons

½ cup (125ml) extra virgin olive oil

salt and freshly ground black pepper

pinch of paprika, for serving

pita bread, for serving

Place drained chickpeas in the bowl of a food processor with garlic and tahini. Process to chop roughly.

Add the juice of one lemon and process to combine. With the motor running, slowly add the olive oil in a thin and steady stream until the mixture is a smooth paste.

Season with salt and pepper, to taste, and add more lemon juice if you like, to taste.

Spoon into in a bowl and sprinkle with a little paprika. Serve with pita bread.

GREEN PEA HUMMUS

Serves 8

2 ½ cups (375g) frozen peas

2 cloves garlic, crushed

1 tsp ground cumin

juice of 1 large lemon

4 tsp extra virgin olive oil

4 tsp tahini (see glossary page 306)

salt

ground paprika, for serving

toasted flat bread, for serving

lemon wedges, for serving

Cook peas in boiling water, until just tender. Drain well.

Place peas in a food processor with garlic, cumin, lemon juice, olive oil and tahini. Blend to a purée. Season to taste with salt, adding more lemon, if needed.

Spoon hummus into a bowl and sprinkle with paprika. Serve with flat bread and lemon wedges.

WHITE BEAN DIP WITH GRILLED VEGETABLES

Serves 6

2 x 14oz (400g) cans
cannellini beans (or other
white beans), rinsed and
drained

3 cloves garlic, crushed

⅓ cup (80ml) extra virgin
olive oil + extra 1 Tbsp, for
serving

juice of 1 lemon

salt

smoked paprika, for serving

Grilled vegetables
1lb (450g) Japanese long
eggplants (aubergines),
halved lengthwise

4 zucchini (courgettes),
sliced lengthwise

2 red bell peppers
(capsicums), deseeded,
quartered lengthwise

2 yellow bell peppers
(capsicums), deseeded,
quartered lengthwise

Blend the drained beans, garlic, extra virgin olive oil
and lemon juice in a food processor until smooth.
Season with salt, to taste.

Spoon dip into a serving bowl. Drizzle with extra oil and
sprinkle with paprika.

To cook grilled vegetables, preheat a chargrill to high heat.

Brush vegetables with olive oil. Grill for 2 to 3 minutes each
side, until tender. Serve vegetables on a platter with white
bean dip.

BELL PEPPER & SUNFLOWER SEED DIP

Serves 6

1 cup (130g) sunflower seeds

3 red bell peppers (capsicums), deseeded and halved

olive oil, for cooking

1 hot red chili, deseeded and coarsely chopped

2 cloves garlic

¼ cup (60ml) olive oil

salt and freshly ground black pepper

Preheat oven to 400°F (200°C).

Spread sunflower seeds in an oven pan and toast in oven for 5 to 7 minutes, stirring once or twice.

Place the bell pepper halves, skin side up, in an oven pan. Rub skins with a little olive oil and roast for 20 minutes, or until skins blister.

Remove peppers from oven and place in a bowl, setting oven pan aside.

Cover peppers with plastic wrap and leave to cool (this allows the peppers to sweat so that their skins peel off easily). Remove and discard skins.

Place bell peppers and any pan juices, along with chili and garlic, in the bowl of a food processor. Blend. Add sunflower seeds and olive oil, and process again until smooth. Season to taste.

Spoon dip into a serving bowl.

SPICED NUTS

Serves 12

2 Tbsp superfine (caster) sugar

1 tsp salt

1 tsp ground cumin

1 tsp ground paprika

1 tsp ground coriander

½ tsp chili powder

1 egg white

3 cups (450g) mixed natural nuts, such as cashews, almonds, walnuts, pecans, peanuts, brazil nuts or pistachios

Preheat oven to 325°F (160°C).

Combine sugar, salt and spices in a small bowl.

In another bowl, whisk egg white until foamy but not stiff. Whisk in sugar and spice mix, then add nuts and stir until well coated.

Spread nuts in a single layer in a baking pan. Bake for 15 minutes, then remove from the oven and stir to separate. Return to the oven for another 5 to 10 minutes, or until golden brown.

Remove from the oven to cool. Break up any nuts that cluster together.

VEGETABLE CRISPS

Serves 4

vegetable oil for deep-frying

1 potato, unpeeled, thinly sliced

1 beet, peeled and thinly sliced

1 carrot, peeled and thinly sliced

1 parsnip, peeled and thinly sliced

3 Tbsp finely chopped parsley

2 tsp sea salt

1 tsp coarsely ground black pepper

Heat oil in a deep-fryer to 350°F (180°C), or in a wok or deep saucepan on high until oil is shimmering.

Pat vegetable slices dry on paper towels.

Deep-fry vegetables in batches for 5 minutes, until golden and crisp. Drain on more paper towels.

In a large bowl, toss together vegetable crisps, parsley, salt and pepper. Serve immediately.

Cook's note If possible, use a mandolin to cut the vegetables into very thin slices.

DOLMADES

Makes 24

¼ cup (60ml) olive oil

1 medium onion, finely chopped

3 Tbsp pine nuts

½ cup (110g) long-grain rice

3 Tbsp currants

½ cup (125ml) water

3 Tbsp finely chopped parsley

2 tsp finely grated lemon zest

24 preserved vine leaves, rinsed and dried

extra virgin olive oil, for serving

feta and olives, for serving

Cooking liquid

¾ cup (180ml) water

3 Tbsp olive oil

4 tsp lemon juice

Heat ¼ cup (60ml) olive oil in a medium-sized saucepan on medium-high heat. Sauté onion for 3 to 4 minutes, until tender. Add pine nuts and cook for 2 to 3 minutes, until lightly browned. Stir in the rice and the currants.

Add ½ cup (125ml) water. Simmer, covered, over low heat for 10 minutes, until the liquid is absorbed into the rice. Remove from heat.

Stir through parsley and lemon zest, and season to taste with salt. Cool.

Place leaves, vein-side up, on a clean work surface. Spoon 1 tablespoon of rice filling onto the end of each leaf. Roll up into a parcel, tucking ends in.

Pack dolmades close together in a single layer in a medium-sized saucepan. Pour in cooking liquid of combined water, olive oil and lemon juice. Weigh down with a plate.

Simmer, covered, for 25 to 30 minutes, until leaves are tender. Cool in pan.

Serve at room temperature drizzled with olive oil, accompanied with feta and olives.

Cook's note Store any leftover vine leaves in the fridge in their original packaging, in the brine, and covered with plastic wrap. They will last for several weeks.

SPANISH TORTILLA

Serves 4 to 6

2lb (1kg) Yukon Gold potatoes (or other waxy potatoes), peeled

¼ cup (60ml) olive oil

1 onion, thinly sliced

6 eggs

salt and freshly ground black pepper

Cook potatoes in a saucepan of boiling salted water for 5 to 10 minutes, until just tender. Drain well and slice.

Heat oil in an 8 to 9 inch (20 to 23 cm) skillet (fry-pan) on medium heat. Add potato slices and onion and sauté for 5 minutes, until tender and golden. Reduce heat to low.

Whisk eggs and season with salt and pepper. Pour into skillet over potato and onion mixture.

Cook tortilla on low heat for 5 to 10 minutes, until base is firm and edges have begun to set.

Loosen edges of tortilla with a metal spatula. Slide it onto a large, flat plate, then flip tortilla carefully onto another plate, and slide it back into same hot pan, uncooked side down. Cook for another 5 minutes, until firm. Transfer to a platter. Stand for 10 minutes before cutting into wedges to serve.

CHICKPEA PATTIES WITH MINT RAITA

Makes 36

1 ½ cups (300g) dried chickpeas

1 onion, finely chopped

2 tsp finely grated ginger

1 clove garlic, crushed

⅓ cup (10g) chopped cilantro (coriander)

1 hot green chili, finely chopped

1 tsp cumin seeds

½ tsp salt

6 curry leaves (optional)

vegetable oil, for cooking

Mint raita

1 cup (30g) roughly chopped mint

1 tsp finely grated ginger

1 clove garlic, crushed

1 cup (225g) unsweetened natural yogurt

Place chickpeas in a large bowl and cover with boiling water. Cover and set aside to soak for 2 hours.

Meanwhile, to make mint raita, combine all ingredients in a small bowl. Cover and refrigerate.

Drain chickpeas, reserving 1 cup (250ml) of soaking water. Process in a food processor, adding a little soaking water, if necessary, to make a smooth paste. Add onion, ginger, garlic, cilantro, chili, cumin, salt and curry leaves, if using. Process until combined.

Heat oil to a depth of 1 inch (2.5 cm) in a heavy-based skillet (fry-pan) until hot, or until a cube of bread sizzles on contact. Shape tablespoons of mixture into small patties. Cook patties for 2 minutes each side, in batches, until golden brown. Drain on paper towels.

Serve patties hot, with mint raita.

CARROT & ZUCCHINI MINI FRITTATAS

Makes 24

4 eggs

⅓ cup (80g) sour cream

2 carrots, peeled and grated

1 large zucchini (courgette), grated

1 tsp finely grated lemon zest

3 Tbsp snipped chives

3 Tbsp grated parmesan

24 radicchio or small lettuce leaves, to serve

Preheat oven to 350°F (180°C). Grease two 12-hole mini muffin pans.

Whisk eggs and sour cream together in a bowl. Stir in carrot, zucchini, lemon zest, chives and parmesan.

Spoon into prepared pans and bake for 15 minutes, until puffed and golden. Cool on a wire rack.

To serve, place each frittata in a small radicchio or lettuce leaf.

VEGETABLE FRITTERS WITH CHILI SAUCE

Makes 20

1 cup (125g) all-purpose (plain) flour

2 tsp salt

1 ½ cups (375ml) water

1 cup (80g) mung bean sprouts

2 celery ribs with their leaves, base trimmed, finely chopped

3 scallions (spring onions), finely sliced on the diagonal, + extra for serving

3 cabbage leaves, finely sliced into 1 inch-long (2.5 cm) strips

2 shallots, finely chopped

1 small Desiree potato (or other all purpose potato), peeled and cut into matchsticks

1 clove garlic, crushed

freshly ground black pepper

½ cup (125ml) vegetable oil chili sauce, for serving

Sift flour and salt into a large bowl. Add water and whisk to make a smooth batter. Add all vegetables, garlic and pepper to taste. Stir just to combine.

Heat oil in a skillet (fry-pan) or wok on medium-high until a cube of bread sizzles on contact. Working in batches, cook 2 tablespoons of batter per fritter, for 2 minutes each side, until golden.

Drain on paper towels. Scatter with extra scallions and serve hot with chili sauce.

MUSHROOM & ARUGULA BRUSCHETTA

Serves 2

vegetable oil spray

4 thick slices ciabatta

1 clove garlic, halved

10oz (300g) small white
mushrooms, halved

1 handful baby arugula
(rocket)

¼ cup (25g) shaved
parmesan

Dressing

3 Tbsp olive oil

4 tsp lemon juice

1 clove garlic, crushed

½ tsp parsley, finely
chopped

½ tsp thyme leaves, finely
chopped

Spray a chargrill with oil and preheat on medium.

Chargrill the bread for 2 to 3 minutes each side, until crisp.
Rub one side of each slice with halved garlic. Set aside.

Chargrill mushrooms for 2 to 3 minutes, until browned and
tender. Remove from pan and cover to keep warm.

To make dressing, whisk olive oil, lemon juice, crushed garlic
and chopped herbs in a small bowl. Season to taste. Spoon
over mushrooms and mix well.

Arrange arugula, mushrooms and parmesan on garlicky side
of grilled bread. Serve immediately.

PEA & LEEK CROSTINI

Serves 8

2 tsp olive oil

2 leeks, white and pale green parts, thinly sliced

¼ cup (60ml) water

salt and freshly ground pepper

1 cup (150g) frozen peas

1 Tbsp extra virgin olive oil

¼ cup (25g) grated parmesan

4 mint leaves, chopped

½ baguette, cut into ¼ inch (6 mm) thick slices

extra mint leaves, for serving

snow pea (mangetout) sprouts, for serving

Heat oil in a non-stick skillet (fry-pan) on medium. Add leek and cook, stirring, for 2 minutes. Add water and reduce heat to a simmer. Season to taste with salt and pepper. Add another ¼ cup (60ml) water if pan becomes dry and leek is not yet soft. Cook until water evaporates.

Meanwhile, blanch peas for 3 minutes in boiling water, until still bright green but softened. Drain, add to leek and stir.

Spoon leek and pea mixture into a food processor. Add olive oil and pulse until coarse.

Add parmesan and mint and process again. Mixture should remain a little chunky. Toast the bread. Spoon pea and leek mixture onto hot toast. Garnish with mint leaves and sprouts. Serve immediately.

BURGERS,
SANDWICHES,
PIZZAS

MAKING GREAT VEGETARIAN SANDWICHES

What could be better than sinking your teeth into a scrumptious, homemade sandwich? With a little creativity, you can have a tasty and nutritious meal in minutes and vegetarian sandwiches make some of the best.

Start with a solid foundation. Bread comes in many shapes, sizes and flavors, so choose something out of the ordinary and experiment with different flavors and textures — pita pockets, wraps, dark rye, focaccia, sourdough, crunchy baguettes, seedy loaves, soft baps, lavosh, naan, bagels…

When it comes to fillings, the options are endless.

Cheese and bread are traditional partners. Experiment with the many varieties available: gruyère, brie, taleggio, mozzarella are great for grilling, while feta and cheddar add a sharp, tasty hit. Don't forget that soft cheeses such as ricotta make great spreads.

Fresh salads make a wholesome filling combined with your favorite dressing — how about a Caesar sandwich?

Roasted and grilled vegetables make tasty fillings, too. Try roasted onion with arugula (rocket) and a splash of balsamic, for example, or build a sandwich around grilled zucchini (courgettes) and peppers (capsicum) & with a touch of ricotta for a wonderful charred flavour.

Dips such as hummus, guacamole, tzatiki and pesto are brilliant building blocks for hearty sandwiches. Spread them thickly, in place of butter.

Egg mayonnaise is a classic but frittatas make great fillings, too. Make a thin frittata, adding a favorite cheese, vegetable and herb combination (asparagus and dill, for example), allow the frittata to cool a little then use it to fill a soft roll, adding a little relish, just like the Italians do!

VEGETABLE BURGERS WITH HUMMUS

Makes 4

1 ½ x 14oz (400g) cans chickpeas, rinsed and drained

3 Tbsp water

¼ cup (60ml) olive oil

1 onion, finely chopped

2 cloves garlic, crushed

1 ½ tsp ground cumin

¼ cup (10g) baby spinach leaves, chopped

½ cup (60g) finely grated cheddar

1 carrot, peeled and grated

2 eggs, lightly beaten

¼ cup (30g) dry breadcrumbs

1 tsp salt

1 tsp freshly ground black pepper

1 loaf Turkish bread (or foccacia), cut into 4, split

½ cup readymade hummus (or see recipe on page 24)

8 slices canned beets

mixed salad leaves, to serve

Place chickpeas and water in a food processor. Process until a coarse paste is formed.

Heat 1 tablespoon of the olive oil in a large skillet (fry-pan) on medium heat. Sauté onion and garlic for 2 to 3 minutes, until soft. Add cumin and cook, stirring, for 1 minute. Mix in spinach. Cook for 1 minute, until spinach begins to wilt, then remove from heat.

In a bowl, combine chickpea paste, onion mixture, cheese, carrot, egg and breadcrumbs. Season with salt and pepper. Shape mixture into 4 evenly sized rectangular patties.

Heat remaining oil in a skillet on medium-high heat. Fry patties for 2 minutes each side, or until golden. Drain on paper towels.

Meanwhile, toast the bread. Spread half the toasted bread with hummus. Next add a patty to each burger, then 2 beet slices and some salad leaves. Top with remaining toasted bread.

TOFU BURGERS WITH THAI SALAD

Makes 8

14oz (400g) can cannellini beans (or other white beans), rinsed and drained

10oz (300g) firm tofu, drained

1½ cups (90g) fresh whole wheat (wholemeal) breadcrumbs

1 red onion, roughly chopped

⅓ cup (10g) mint leaves

⅓ cup (10g) cilantro (coriander) leaves

1 egg, lightly beaten

2 Tbsp readymade teriyaki marinade

1 clove garlic, crushed

¼ cup (35g) all-purpose (plain) flour

¼ tsp baking powder

2 Tbsp vegetable oil

8 Turkish rolls (or other white rolls), split

1 cup (40g) alfalfa sprouts, for serving

½ cup (15g) cilantro (coriander) leaves, for serving

Thai salad

3 plum (roma) tomatoes, finely chopped

3 Tbsp chopped cilantro (coriander)

1 small red chili, finely chopped

3 Tbsp lime juice

1 tsp light brown (soft brown) sugar

Place beans, tofu, breadcrumbs, onion, herbs, egg, teriyaki marinade and garlic in a food processor. Process until smooth. Add flour and baking powder and blend to combine. Transfer mixture to a large bowl, cover with plastic wrap and refrigerate until well chilled.

To make the salad, combine all ingredients in a bowl.

Heat oil in a medium skillet (fry-pan) on high. Divide mixture roughly into 8, scooping each portion into the pan using a large serving spoon. Cook burgers for 2 to 3 minutes each side, until firm and golden. Drain on paper towels. Meanwhile, toast rolls.

Serve patties on rolls and top with salad, alfalfa sprouts and cilantro leaves, with any remaining salsa served on the side.

LENTIL BURGERS WITH BELL PEPPERS & CREAM CHEESE

Makes 4

cooking oil spray

1 small red onion, finely chopped

14oz (400g) can lentils, rinsed and drained

3 Tbsp chopped parsley

3 Tbsp all-purpose (plain) flour

1 egg, beaten

½ tsp salt

4 whole wheat (wholemeal) buns, split

¼ cup (60g) cream cheese

1½ cups (270g) chargrilled bell pepper (capsicum), thinly sliced

1 cup (40g) alfafa sprouts

Spray a thin layer of oil in a heavy skillet (fry-pan) and place on medium heat. Sauté onion for 2 to 3 minutes, until soft. Transfer to a bowl with a quarter of the lentils.

Blend remaining lentils with parsley, flour, egg and salt in afood processor, until smooth. Add to bowl with onion mixture, and stir to combine. Cover with plastic wrap and refrigerate to chill.

Wipe out skillet with a paper towel. Spray with oil again and place on medium heat. Divide lentil mixture into 4 equal portions and flatten to form patties with a metal spatula. Cook for 2 to 3 minutes each side, until crisp and golden.

Spread base of buns with cream cheese. Top with patties, pepper slices and alfafa. Serve with other half of bun.

MEXICAN BEAN BURGERS

Makes 4

14oz (400g) can red kidney beans, rinsed and drained

11oz (300g) vegetarian sausage-meat substitute

4oz (125g) can sweetcorn kernels, drained

2 scallions (spring onions), finely sliced

⅓ cup (40g) dry breadcrumbs

1 egg, lightly beaten

½ cup (15g) chopped cilantro (coriander) leaves

½ tsp ground cumin

2 tsp vegetable oil

2 English muffins, split

½ avocado, sliced

2 tomatoes, cut into wedges, for serving

lettuce leaves, for serving

Yogurt dressing

⅓ cup (80ml) unsweetened natural yogurt

¼ tsp salt

2 Tbsp extra cilantro (coriander) leaves

Pulse drained beans in food processor until coarsely chopped. Transfer beans to a large mixing bowl and add vegetarian sausage-meat, sweetcorn, scallion, breadcrumbs, egg, cilantro and cumin. Mix well.

Shape mixture into 8 patties. Cover with plastic wrap and refrigerate to chill.

To make yogurt dressing, combine yogurt, salt and cilantro and set aside.

Heat vegetable oil in a skillet (fry-pan) on medium heat. Cook patties for 3 to 4 minutes each side, until golden.

Meanwhile, toast muffins. Top one half of each muffin with a patty and sliced avocado. Finish with yogurt dressing. Serve tomato and lettuce on the side.

MUSHROOM BURGERS

Makes 4

olive oil, for cooking

1lb (450g) small white mushrooms, thinly sliced

1 large onion, finely diced

2 cloves garlic, crushed

1 egg, lightly beaten

2 cups (120g) fresh breadcrumbs

salt and freshly ground black pepper

4 burger buns, split

salad leaves, for serving

chutney or relish, for serving

Heat 2 tablespoons olive oil in a heavy skillet (fry-pan). Add mushrooms and onion and sauté over medium heat for 5 minutes, until the pan juices evaporate and the mushrooms are lightly browned. Blend half this mixture in a food processor.

Place cooked mushrooms and mushroom purée in a mixing bowl with the garlic, egg and fresh breadcrumbs. Season with salt and pepper and mix well to combine.

Divide mixture into 4 and shape into patties. Cover with plastic wrap and refrigerate to chill.

Heat 2 tablespoons olive oil in skillet, add mushroom patties and cook over a medium heat for 4 to 5 minutes on each side. Drain on paper towels.

Meanwhile, toast burger buns and place bases on serving plates. Top each one with salad and a mushroom patty, then top with the bun lids. Serve with chutney.

FALAFEL & PITA WITH GARLIC YOGURT SAUCE

Makes 4

Garlic yogurt sauce

1 cup (225g) unsweetened, thick-style yogurt

2 cloves garlic, crushed

2 Tbsp chopped fresh mint

pinch of chili powder

Falafel

olive oil, for cooking

13oz (375g) readymade falafel mixture (available from delis and supermarkets)

4 large rounds of pita bread

2 cups (60g) loosely packed arugula (rocket) or other small salad leaves

4oz (125g) cherry tomatoes, halved

To make garlic yogurt sauce, combine all the ingredients in a small bowl.

Heat oil in a skillet (fry pan) over a medium heat. Next, drop tablespoonfuls of the falafel mixture into the oil and shallow-fry in batches for 2 to 3 minutes on each side, until well browned. Drain falafel patties on paper towels.

Meanwhile, warm pita breads in toaster or oven.

Arrange arugula and tomatoes on pita. Add falafel. Spoon garlic yogurt sauce on top.

SWEET POTATO & MINT WRAP

Makes 4

1lb (450g) sweet potato, peeled and thinly sliced

7oz (200g) feta, diced

3½ oz (100g) cream cheese

¼ tsp salt

freshly ground black pepper

4 whole wheat (wholemeal) wraps

1 small red onion, finely sliced

½ cup (15g) shredded mint leaves

Preheat oven to 400°F (200°C). Lightly grease a large roasting tray.

Spread sweet potato slices on prepared tray. Roast for 10 to 15 minutes, until tender.

In a bowl, mix feta and cream cheese until smooth. Season with salt and pepper.

Spread feta mixture on each wrap. Scatter with onion and mint. Place sweet potato slices on top. Roll up. Cut in half crosswise and serve.

CHARGRILLED VEGETABLE QUESADILLAS WITH TOMATO SALSA

Makes 4

1 cup (180g) chargrilled bell pepper (capsicum), chopped

1 cup (150g) chargrilled eggplant (aubergine), chopped

1 cup (100g) semi-dried tomatoes, chopped

8 small flour tortillas

2 cups (250g) grated mozzarella

½ cup (15g) shredded basil

4 tsp olive oil

Tomato salsa

2 plum (roma) tomatoes, finely chopped

1 small red onion, finely chopped

3 Tbsp shredded basil

2 tsp lemon juice

2 tsp olive oil

½ tsp salt

In a small bowl, combine the bell pepper, eggplant and semi-dried tomato.

Place 4 tortillas on a clean work surface and arrange ¼ cup (30g) of cheese on each. Top evenly with vegetable mixture, basil and remaining cheese. Cover with remaining tortillas.

Heat 1 tsp oil in a heavy skillet (fry-pan). Cook quesadillas one at a time (adding 1 tsp of oil before each) for 2 to 3 minutes each side, until lightly browned and cheese has melted. Remove from pan and cover to keep warm.

To make the tomato salsa, combine all the ingredients in a small bowl.

Cut quesadillas into wedges and serve with tomato salsa.

POTATO & ROSEMARY PIZZA

Makes 1

1 quantity pizza dough (see glossary, page 310)

2 Tbsp olive oil

1 large potato, thinly sliced

1 clove garlic, crushed

2 tsp chopped rosemary leaves + extra leaves, for serving

salt and freshly ground black pepper

Preheat oven to 400°F (200°C). Lightly grease a pizza or baking sheet.

Using a rolling pin, roll dough into a 12 inch (30 cm) round. Place on prepared sheet. Brush dough with a little of the oil.

In a large bowl, combine potato slices, garlic, rosemary and remaining oil. Toss gently to combine, and season with salt and pepper.

Arrange slices neatly over pizza base.

Bake 25 to 30 minutes, until cooked and golden. Top with extra rosemary leaves. Slice into wedges to serve.

MUSHROOM, BLUE CHEESE & THYME PIZZA

Makes 1

1 quantity pizza dough (see glossary, page 310)

2 Tbsp olive oil

2 cloves garlic, crushed

3 ½ oz (100g) small portabella mushrooms, sliced

3 ½ oz (100g) blue cheese, thinly sliced or crumbled

few sprigs of thyme

salt and freshly ground black pepper

Preheat oven to 400°F (200°C). Lightly grease a pizza or baking sheet.

Using a rolling pin, roll dough into a 12 inch (30 cm) round. Place on prepared sheet. Combine oil and garlic, and use a little to brush pizza base.

Scatter mushrooms, cheese and thyme over base. Season with salt and pepper.

Bake for 15 to 20 minutes, or until crust is golden brown and crisp. Slice into wedges to serve.

BREAKFASTS & SUPPERS

RANCH EGGS WITH TOMATOES

Serves 2

1 Tbsp olive oil

1 small red onion, finely chopped

¼ tsp chili powder

½ tsp ground cumin

14oz (400g) can diced tomatoes

14oz (400g) can black-eyed peas, rinsed and drained

salt and freshly ground black pepper

2 eggs

2 Tbsp chopped cilantro (coriander) or parsley, for serving

toast, for serving

Heat oil in a medium-sized skillet (fry-pan). Add onion and cook for 5 minutes over a medium heat until soft. Add the spices, then cook for a further minute.

Add tomatoes and bring to a boil, then reduce heat and simmer for 5 minutes. Add the drained peas and simmer for 5 minutes. Season with salt and pepper, to taste.

Break each egg into a cup, then slide gently into tomato mixture. Cover and simmer for 5 minutes, or until the eggs are cooked to your liking.

Scatter with fresh herbs and serve with toast.

BEANS ON TOAST

Serves 4

1 Tbsp olive oil

1 onion, diced

2 tsp Spanish smoked paprika

14oz (400g) can kidney beans, rinsed and drained

14oz (400g) can butter beans, rinsed and drained

14oz (400g) can diced tomatoes

½ cup (90g) chopped chargrilled bell pepper (capsicum)

3 Tbsp chopped parsley

3 Tbsp chopped oregano

salt and freshly ground black pepper

4 thick slices toast, for serving

Heat oil in a large skillet (fry-pan) on medium heat. Sauté onion and paprika for 3 to 5 minutes, until onion softens.

Add both beans, the tomatoes and bell pepper. Cook on low heat, stirring occasionally, for 10 minutes, until the sauce thickens.

Stir parsley and oregano into beans. Season to taste. Serve the beans on toast.

TOMATO & CHEDDAR OMELET

Serves 1

2 eggs

2 Tbsp water

salt and freshly ground
black pepper

1 Tbsp butter

1 scallion (spring onion),
finely sliced

1 small tomato, diced

¼ cup (30g) grated
cheddar

Break eggs into a bowl, add water, season with salt and pepper and whisk to combine.

Heat butter in a non-stick skillet (fry-pan) over a medium heat until the butter sizzles. Pour in the egg mixture. Draw the mixture away from the sides of the pan towards the center as it cooks, using a wooden spatula.

When the egg mixture is nearly cooked, add the scallion, tomato and cheddar to the center of the omelet. Flip one side of the omelet over the other, then gently slide the omelet onto a plate, to serve.

FETA, PEA & MINT FRITTATA

Serves 6

1 Tbsp (15g) butter

1 leek, thinly sliced

3 scallions (spring onions), thinly sliced

3 ½ oz (100g) feta, crumbled

1 cup (150g) frozen peas

⅓ cup (10g) chopped mint

6 eggs

1 cup (250ml) milk

¼ cup (35g) all-purpose (plain) flour

1 tsp salt

freshly ground black pepper

Preheat oven to 400°F (200°C). Line an 11 x 7 inch (18 x 28 cm) pan with parchment paper.

Melt butter in a skillet (fry-pan) on medium heat. Add leek and scallions and cook for 4 minutes, until leek softens. Spread into prepared pan and scatter feta, peas and mint over leeks.

Whisk together eggs, milk, flour, salt and pepper. Pour egg mixture over vegetable mixture. Bake for 30 minutes, until eggs are set and the frittata is golden. Serve hot or cold, cut into squares.

BAKED EGGS WITH SPINACH & PARMESAN

Serves 2

butter, for greasing

4 eggs

2 Tbsp cream

1/3 cup (10g) finely chopped spinach leaves

1/4 cup (25g) grated parmesan

salt and freshly ground black pepper

toast, for serving

Preheat oven to 350°F (180°C). Grease two small ramekins generously with butter.

Break eggs into a bowl, add cream, spinach and parmesan and whisk to combine. Season well with salt and pepper.

Pour mixture into prepared ramekins, dividing evenly. Place ramekins in an oven pan and fill pan with enough hot water to come halfway up the sides of the ramekins.

Place in the oven to bake for 15 minutes, or until eggs are just set. Serve with toast.

ZUCCHINI PANCAKES WITH BRIE

Serves 4

2 cups (250g) grated zucchini (courgettes)

½ cup (125ml) milk

2 eggs, lightly beaten

4 Tbsp (60g) butter, melted

½ cup (65g) all-purpose (plain) flour, sifted

½ cup (45g) grated parmesan

3 Tbsp chopped parsley

1 clove garlic, crushed

½ tsp grated nutmeg

½ tsp salt

4oz (125g) brie, thinly sliced

4oz (100g) semi-dried tomatoes

3 Tbsp snipped chives

freshly ground black pepper, to serve

Squeeze zucchini in a colander to remove any excess liquid. Place in a large bowl. Stir in milk, egg and butter. Fold in flour, parmesan, parsley, garlic, nutmeg and salt. Combine mixture until smooth.

Heat a non-stick skillet (fry-pan) to medium heat. Working in batches, add ¼ cup (60ml) measures of zucchini mixture, leaving room for spreading, and cook for 2 minutes each side, until golden. Stack pancakes on a plate and keep warm while cooking remaining batter.

To serve, top pancakes with brie, semi-dried tomatoes, and a sprinkling of chives and freshly ground pepper.

FAVA BEAN PUFFS

Makes 8

¾ stick (90g) butter + extra for greasing ramekins

⅓ cup (45g) all-purpose (plain) flour + extra for dusting ramekins

1lb (450g) frozen double-peeled fava beans (broad beans)

1 ½ cups (375ml) milk

8oz (225g) chèvre (goats cheese), crumbled

4 eggs, separated

Preheat oven to 450°F (230°C). Butter and flour eight ¾ cup (180ml) capacity ramekins.

Cook fava beans in a saucepan of boiling salted water for 1 minute. Drain. Cool in ice-cold water. Drain again.

Place beans and ¾ cup (180ml) milk in food processor and blend until smooth.

Melt butter in a small saucepan on medium heat. Add flour and cook, stirring, for 1 minute. Whisk in remaining milk until smooth. Transfer to a large bowl. Whisk bean mixture into flour mixture. Add chèvre, egg yolks and salt, beating to combine well.

Using an electric beater, beat egg whites to stiff, glossy peaks. Gently fold egg whites through bean mixture in two batches.

Spoon into prepared ramekins and bake puffs for 20 to 25 minutes, until risen and golden. Serve immediately.

THAI SON-IN-LAW EGGS

Serves 4

4oz (120g) palm sugar, grated (see glossary, page 307)

¼ cup (60ml) light soy sauce

3 Tbsp tamarind purée (see glossary, page 307)

2 shallots, thinly sliced

⅓ cup (80ml) water

2 cups (500ml) vegetable oil

3 cloves garlic, sliced lengthwise

½ hot red chili, finely sliced

4 eggs

½ small cabbage, shredded

1 bunch cilantro (coriander), washed and divided into sprigs

steamed jasmine rice, for serving

In a small saucepan on medium heat, stir sugar, soy sauce, tamarind, half of the chopped shallot, and water, until sugar has dissolved. Reduce heat to low and simmer for 10 minutes, until syrupy. Strain into a bowl, set aside.

Heat oil in a wok on medium heat. Fry remaining shallot, garlic and chili for 20 seconds, until crisp. Remove from pan using a slotted spoon.

In the same hot oil, fry eggs one by one. Slide each egg carefully into the oil, avoiding splatters. Cook for 30 seconds, turn and fry for another 30 seconds, until puffed and golden. Drain on paper towels.

Arrange cabbage in bowls. Top with eggs, spoon over sauce and top with fried shallot mixture and cilantro. Serve with rice.

Cook's note The tartness of the sauce in this dish is said to be a reminder to a son-in-law that any bad behavior has been noted!

VEGETABLE & NOODLE OMELET

Serves 2

3 eggs

2 scallions (spring onions), chopped

2oz (60g) thin dried egg noodles, soaked until softened, and drained

2 tsp vegetable oil

6 fresh or canned baby corn, halved lengthwise

½ red bell pepper (capsicum), deseeded and sliced

1 Tbsp hoisin sauce

¼ cup (20g) mung bean sprouts

¼ cup (10g) cilantro (coriander) leaves, for serving

extra chopped scallion (spring onion), for serving

chopped red chili, for serving

In a large bowl, whisk together eggs and scallion. Stir in egg noodles.

Heat vegetable oil in an 8 inch (20 cm) non-stick skillet (fry-pan) over medium-low heat.

Add egg mixture to pan, tilting to cover base evenly. Cook for 5 to 6 minutes, until edges of omelet have set and underside is golden.

Scatter baby corn and red pepper over the omelet. Cover with a lid and cook for further 3 to 4 minutes, until vegetables are tender and omelet is firm. Spoon over hoisin sauce.

Serve omelet topped with mung bean sprouts, cilantro and scallion. Place chopped chili in a small side dish to add to taste.

SELF-CRUSTING BROCCOLI & PINE NUT TART

Serves 6

butter, for greasing

1lb (450g) broccoli

3 scallions (spring onions), sliced

1 cup (125g) grated cheddar, or other strong cheese

4 eggs

1 cup (250ml) milk

½ cup (65g) all-purpose (plain) flour

½ tsp baking powder

½ tsp salt

freshly ground black pepper

1 Tbsp chopped oregano

⅓ cup (40g) pine nuts

Preheat oven to 400°F (200°C). Grease a ceramic quiche dish with butter.

Cut the broccoli into bite-sized florets and cook in boiling, salted water for 3 minutes, then drain well. Scatter broccoli over the base of the dish. Add scallion and grated cheese.

Beat eggs in a bowl, add milk, flour and baking powder, whisking to combine. Stir in salt, pepper and oregano.

Pour egg mixture into the quiche dish and scatter with pine nuts. Bake for 25 to 30 minutes, or until golden brown and set. Allow to cool slightly.

Serve warm, cut in wedges.

RED WINE MUSHROOM RAGOÛT

Serves 4

⅔ stick (80g) butter

¼ cup (60ml) extra virgin olive oil

8 cloves garlic, crushed

4 scallions (spring onions), finely sliced

9oz (250g) small white mushrooms

9oz (250g) brown mushrooms

2 tsp thyme leaves

½ tsp salt

freshly ground black pepper

1 cup (250ml) red wine

buttered toast, for serving

½ cup (15g) chopped parsley

Heat butter and oil in a heavy-based medium saucepan to medium heat. Add garlic, scallion, mushrooms and thyme to pan; season with salt and pepper. Cover saucepan and cook for 10 minutes, without stirring.

Remove lid, increase heat to high and add wine. Bring to boil, then reduce heat and simmer for a further 10 minutes, until mushrooms are tender.

Serve ragoût on toast, sprinkled with parsley.

ROASTED VIDALIA ONIONS WITH BLUE CHEESE

Serves 4

4 large Vidalia onions (or other sweet onions), peeled, cut into 1 inch (2.5 cm) thick slices

¼ cup (60ml) extra virgin olive oil

2 tsp salt

4oz (125g) blue cheese, crumbled

4 tsp red wine vinegar

½ cup (65g) chopped walnuts

⅓ cup (10g) snipped chives

crusty bread, for serving

Preheat oven to 400°F (200°C). Line a baking sheet with parchment paper.

Place onion slices on lined baking sheet and brush with half the oil. Season with salt. Roast for 30 minutes. Turn onion slices over and cook for another 10 minutes, until tender and edges are browned.

Transfer to a warmed platter, scatter with cheese and drizzle with remaining oil and then vinegar. Sprinkle with walnuts and chives. Serve with crusty bread.

SOUPS

GAZPACHO

Serves 6

4 medium-sized ripe tomatoes, peeled and chopped

1 ½ red bell peppers (capsicums), deseeded and chopped

1 long cucumber, peeled and chopped

3 small red onions

2 cloves garlic, sliced

¼ baguette, crusts removed, broken into pieces

¼ cup (60ml) extra virgin olive oil

2 Tbsp white wine vinegar

½ teaspoon minced hot chili

¼ tsp sugar

1 ½ cups (375ml) water

salt

2 thick slices white bread, crusts removed

1 small handful of ice cubes

small croutons, for serving

Set aside one fourth of the chopped tomato, bell pepper, cucumber and onion in a bowl. Place remainder in a large bowl, and add garlic, bread, oil, vinegar, chili and sugar. Cover with water. Season to taste with salt. Combine well. Cover with plastic wrap and refrigerate for at least 3 hours.

Meanwhile, make croutons by toasting bread and cutting it into cubes.

Transfer cold tomato mixture to a food processor or blender. Add ice cubes, and process until smooth. Strain to remove pieces of skin, pressing well to get all the liquid through the sieve.

Pour into serving glasses. Serve topped with a spoonful of the reserved tomato, bell pepper, cucumber and onion and some croutons.

CHILLED CUCUMBER SOUP WITH PISTACHIO & DILL

Serves 4

1lb (450g) long cucumbers, peeled and coarsely grated

1 clove garlic, crushed

1 tsp ground cumin

2 cups (450g) unsweetened natural yogurt

½ cup (125ml) vegetable stock + extra in reserve

salt

3 Tbsp chopped pistachios, for serving

3 Tbsp dill sprigs, for serving

Blend cucumber, garlic, cumin and yogurt in a food processor, until smooth.

Transfer to a mixing bowl and stir in stock, adding more if soup is too thick. Season to taste.

Cover soup and refrigerate for at least 30 minutes, to chill.

Serve soup topped with pistachios and dill.

HOT & SOUR SOUP WITH TOFU

Serves 4

6 cups (1.5L) vegetable stock

2 stalks lemongrass, crushed

1 inch (2.5 cm) piece fresh ginger, peeled and finely grated

12oz (350g) block firm tofu, cut in 1 inch (2.5 cm) cubes

2 large bok choy, trimmed and sliced crosswise

14oz (400g) can baby corn, drained

1 long red chili, finely sliced

juice of 2 limes

¼ cup (10g) cilantro (coriander) leaves, roughly chopped

Place stock, lemongrass and ginger in a large saucepan and bring to a boil on a high heat, then reduce heat and simmer for 5 minutes to allow flavors to infuse. Strain into a bowl to remove lemongrass and ginger. Return stock to the saucepan.

Add tofu and vegetables, then simmer for 5 minutes to heat tofu. Add chili and lime juice. Serve garnished with cilantro.

ROAST TOMATO & BELL PEPPER SOUP

Serves 6

2 red bell peppers (capsicums), halved and deseeded

2 jalapeños (or other medium hot chilies), halved and deseeded

2lb (900g) plum (roma) tomatoes, halved

3 Tbsp olive oil

salt and freshly ground black pepper

¼ cup (10g) tarragon leaves

1 Tbsp (15g) butter

1 onion, chopped

2 cloves garlic, crushed

4 cups (1L) vegetable stock

2 large Desiree potatoes (or other all-purpose potatoes), peeled and chopped

½ cup (115g) sour cream, for serving

Preheat oven to 350°F (180°C).

Place bell peppers, jalapeños and tomatoes skin-side up in a roasting pan. Drizzle with oil, season with salt and pepper and scatter tarragon leaves on top. Roast for 35 to 40 minutes, or until skins have blistered. Remove from oven.

Place bell peppers and jalapeños in a bowl and cover with plastic wrap, to loosen skins. Set tomatoes aside in pan. When cool, peel skin from tomatoes, peppers and jalapeños.

Melt butter in a large saucepan over medium heat. Sauté onion and garlic for 3 to 4 minutes, until soft. Add stock and potatoes and bring to a boil. Reduce heat and simmer for 10 minutes.

Add cooled roasted vegetables and simmer for a further 10 minutes, or until potatoes are tender.

Pureé soup using a hand blender or food processor. Gently reheat soup. Serve topped with a dollop of sour cream.

PEA VELVET SOUP

Serves 4

1 Tbsp (15g) butter

3 leeks, white parts only, chopped

1 medium onion, finely chopped

5 cups (1.25L) vegetable stock

3 cups (450g) frozen peas

2 large Russet potatoes (or other floury potatoes), peeled and diced

1 tsp salt

Melt the butter in a large saucepan over low heat. Add leek and onion and cook gently for 5 minutes, until soft but not colored.

Add stock, peas, potato and salt. Bring to a boil, reduce heat and simmer for 15 minutes, until tender.

Pureé using a hand blender until very smooth. Reheat soup gently to serve.

ROASTED CARROT & PARSNIP SOUP

Serves 4

6 medium-sized carrots, peeled and chopped

2 parsnips, peeled and chopped

1 leek, white part only, chopped

3 Tbsp olive oil

4 tsp chili paste

4 cups (1L) vegetable stock

13 ½ fl oz (400ml) can light coconut milk

2 tsp light soy sauce

salt and freshly ground black pepper

½ cup (15g) chopped cilantro (coriander), to serve

Preheat oven to 400°F (200°C). Line a large roasting pan with parchment paper.

Place vegetables in prepared pan, add 2 Tbsp of the oil and toss together to coat. Bake for 35 to 40 minutes, until tender.

Heat remaining oil in a large saucepan on medium heat. Add chili paste. Cook, stirring, for 1 minute, until fragrant.

Add roasted vegetables to saucepan, along with stock, coconut milk and soy sauce. Bring to boil. Reduce heat to low. Simmer for 10 minutes.

Using a hand blender, pureé the soup until smooth. Season with salt and pepper, to taste. Serve in bowls and scatter chopped cilantro over the top.

BORSCHT

Serves 6

4 large beets

2 Tbsp olive oil

1 large onion, roughly chopped

2 cloves garlic, chopped

4 cups (1L) vegetable stock

2 tsp white wine vinegar

salt and freshly ground black pepper

½ cup (115g) sour cream, for serving

dill sprigs, for serving

Cook beets whole in boiling water until tender (this may take up to an hour). Drain and remove to cool.

Once beets are cool enough to handle, rub to remove skins. Roughly chop beets.

Heat oil in a large saucepan on low heat, add onion and cook for 5 to 10 minutes to soften. Add garlic and cook for 1 minute more.

Add chopped beet and stock and bring to a boil, then turn down the heat and simmer for 5 minutes. Stir in vinegar.

Purée soup until smooth. Season with salt and pepper, to taste. Reheat, then serve garnished with a dollop of sour cream and a sprig of dill.

MUSHROOM MISO SOUP

Serves 4

6 cups (1.5L) water

⅓ cup (80ml) tamari (see glossary, page 306)

3 Tbsp mirin (see glossary, page 306)

2 tsp sesame oil

3 ½ oz (100g) fresh shiitake mushrooms, thinly sliced

2 Tbsp white miso paste

¼ oz (10g) wakame (dried seaweed)

2 cups (60g) baby spinach leaves

10oz (300g) firm tofu, cut into ½ inch (1.2 cm) cubes

2oz (60g) enokitake mushrooms

¼ cup (25g) sliced scallions (spring onions), for serving

Combine water, tamari and mirin in a large saucepan. Bring to a boil; simmer, uncovered, for 2 minutes.

Meanwhile, heat sesame oil in a medium pan. Add shiitake mushrooms. Cook, stirring, until soft. Remove from heat.

Stir miso and wakame into liquid, then add shiitake mushrooms. Simmer for 2 minutes. Add spinach and cook, stirring, for 2 minutes.

Divide tofu among serving bowls. Ladle miso soup into bowls. Scatter enokitake mushrooms and scallions on top of soup.

MILDLY SPICED LENTIL TOMATO SOUP

Serves 4

1 cup (200g) split yellow lentils, rinsed and drained

1 Tbsp vegetable oil

1 tsp ground turmeric

2 cloves garlic, crushed

10 cups (2.5L) water

3 large tomatoes, chopped

salt

¼ cup (10g) chopped cilantro (coriander)

juice of ½ lemon

1 Tbsp garam masala (see glossary, page 307)

Place lentils, oil, turmeric, garlic and water in a large saucepan. Bring to the boil over high heat, then reduce heat to low and simmer with lid on for 30 to 35 minutes, until lentils are very soft. Add more water, if needed, to keep mixture of a soup consistency.

Add chopped tomato and simmer for another 25 minutes. Season to taste with salt. Stir through cilantro, lemon juice and garam masala before serving.

CAULIFLOWER CREAM SOUP

Serves 6

2 Tbsp olive oil

2 Tbsp butter

1 onion, chopped

1 head of cauliflower, roughly chopped

1 large Russet potato (or other waxy potato), peeled and roughly chopped

3 cups (750ml) vegetable stock

2 cups (500ml) milk

¼ cup (60ml) cream

salt and freshly ground black pepper

⅓ cup (40g) toasted pine nuts, for serving

Heat oil and butter in a large, heavy-based saucepan. Add the onion and cook over a low heat for 5 minutes, to soften. Add cauliflower, potato, stock and milk and bring to a boil over high heat.

Turn down the heat and simmer for 15 minutes, or until vegetables are very soft. Purée the mixture, then return to the pan to reheat.

Stir in cream and season with salt and pepper, to taste. Serve scattered with pine nuts.

TOMATO, POTATO & PESTO SOUP

Serves 4

2 Tbsp olive oil

1 large onion, finely diced

1 bay leaf

4 thyme sprigs

2lb (450g) Desiree potatoes (or other all purpose potatoes), peeled and diced

2 x 14oz (400g) cans chopped tomatoes

2 cups (500ml) water

salt and freshly ground black pepper

6 Tbsp basil pesto, for serving (see page 14)

Heat oil in a large, heavy-based saucepan. Add onion, bay leaf and thyme and cook over a medium heat for 5 to 10 minutes, to soften onion.

Add potatoes, tomatoes and water and bring to a boil over a high heat. Reduce heat and simmer for 15 minutes, until potatoes are tender and flavors are concentrated.

Remove bay leaf and thyme and season with salt and pepper, to taste. Serve topped with a generous dollop of basil pesto.

ZUCCHINI & TARRAGON SOUP

Serves 6

2 tsp olive oil

1 large onion, chopped

3 medium Russet potatoes (or other floury potatoes), peeled, chopped

2 cups (500ml) vegetable stock

2 cups (500ml) water

2lb (900g) zucchini (courgette), chopped

2 tsp chopped tarragon

salt and freshly ground black pepper

Heat olive oil in a medium-sized saucepan on medium heat. Cook onion for 3 minutes, stirring, until soft.

Stir in potato. Add stock and water. Increase heat, bring to a boil, then reduce heat to low and simmer for 5 minutes.

Add zucchini and 1 tsp chopped tarragon. Simmer for 5 minutes.

Using a hand blender, blend zucchini mixture until smooth. Season to taste with salt.

Serve scattered with the remaining tarragon and a good grinding of pepper.

MUSHROOM GOW GEE IN BROTH

Serves 4

4oz (100g) shiitake mushrooms, finely chopped

1 scallion (spring onion), finely chopped

1 tsp Thai sweet chili sauce

1 clove garlic, crushed

½ tsp chili paste

20 round gow gee wrappers

3 cups (750ml) vegetable stock

3 cups (750ml) water

2 inch (5 cm) piece fresh ginger, cut in matchsticks

3 cloves garlic, sliced

3 Tbsp soy sauce

1lb (450g) choy sum, stems sliced, leaves roughly chopped

Combine shiitake, scallion, sweet chili sauce, crushed garlic and chili paste in a bowl.

Place a heaped teaspoon of mushroom mixture onto center of each gow gee wrapper. Brush edges with a little water, fold to enclose filling and crimp edges together to seal.

Place stock and water in a large saucepan with ginger, sliced garlic and soy sauce. Bring to a boil on high, then reduce heat to low and simmer for 10 minutes.

Add gow gee and choy sum to saucepan and simmer for another 5 minutes. Ladle gow gee and broth into bowls.

APPETIZERS

ENTERTAINING MENU
TAPAS AND ANTIPASTI

Often, the most successful entertaining is a casual affair. Take a leaf from the Italian book, and prepare plates of antipasti to share over drinks, or do it the Spanish way, offering a selection of little tapas (snacks). If you make enough, this type of entertaining can take the place of a full meal.

One of the great things about entertaining this way is that you can prepare most things in advance, allowing you to better enjoy the company of your guests.

Arrange the dishes on a table or serving area. Each guest will need a small plate and a fork — and a suitable drink!

Tapas menu
- Gazpacho
- Spanish tortilla
- Swiss chard and cheese pastries
- Red wine mushroom ragoût
- Fresh, crusty bread, to serve

Antipasto menu
- Artichoke pâté with raw vegetables
- Grilled zucchini salad with mint
- Pea and leek crostini
- Mushroom and arugula bruschetta
- Eggplant rotolo

If the event is to be a long affair you might like to finish things with a sweet offering such as good quality, readymade panforte or nougat from your local deli.

COOKING CLASS | GINGER PUMPKIN TRIANGLES

GINGER PUMPKIN TRIANGLES

Makes 9

1 Tbsp olive oil

2 cups (240g) finely diced pie pumpkin

3 Tbsp pine nuts

4 tsp finely grated ginger

1 Tbsp finely chopped jalapeño

2 garlic cloves, crushed

¼ cup (10g) chopped cilantro (coriander)

6 sheets filo pastry

4 Tbsp (60g) butter, melted

Preheat oven to 350°F (180°C). Lightly grease a baking sheet.

STEP 1 Heat oil in a skillet (fry-pan) on medium heat. Sauté the pumpkin for 8 minutes, until tender. Add pine nuts, ginger, chili and garlic. Cook, stirring, for 2 minutes. Mix in cilantro.

STEP 2 Working with two sheets of filo at a time, place on a clean work surface. Brush top side of pastry with butter. Cut lengthwise into 3 even-sized strips. Place a heaped teaspoon of mixture on one end of each pastry strip.

STEP 3 Fold pastry and filling over to form a triangle. Continue folding, keeping triangular shape, until end of strip.

STEP 4 Arrange triangles on tray. Brush with butter. Repeat with remaining pastry and filling.

Bake for 10 to 15 minutes, until golden and crisp. Serve warm.

TOFU NOODLE SPOONS

Makes 30

1 Tbsp Thai sweet chili sauce

1 Tbsp soy sauce

1 clove garlic, crushed

3½ oz (100g) firm tofu, cut into ½ inch (1.2 cm) cubes

12oz (350g) dried egg noodles

1 scallion (spring onion), thinly sliced on the diagonal

1 long red chili, cut into thin strips

Dressing

¼ cup (60ml) soy sauce

1 Tbsp finely grated ginger

juice and grated zest of 1 lime

1 Tbsp light brown (soft brown) sugar

Combine sweet chili sauce, soy and garlic in a shallow dish. Add tofu and gently turn to coat. Set aside for 15 minutes.

Prepare noodles according to packet directions. Drain and place in a large bowl.

To make dressing, whisk together ingredients in a small bowl until sugar dissolves. Pour over warm noodles and toss to combine.

Divide noodles evenly between spoons, twirling a small bundle into each spoon. Lay a cube of marinated tofu on each. Serve topped with scallion and chili.

BELL PEPPER & HALOUMI PARCELS

Serves 4

4 red bell peppers
(capsicums)

7oz (200g) haloumi, cut
into 4 even slices

⅓ cup (80g) olive tapenade

¼ cup (10g) loosely packed
basil leaves

juice and grated zest of
1 lemon

Preheat chargrill to high.

Cook peppers on grill for 15 to 20 minutes, turning frequently,
until the skin blackens and blisters, and the flesh is tender.
Immediatey place peppers in a bowl and cover with plastic
wrap. Set aside to cool. Peel peppers and cut each one in half
lengthwise, then remove skins, seeds and membrane.

Reduce grill heat to medium.

Place each slice of haloumi on a half pepper. Top haloumi with
one-fourth of tapenade, basil leaves and lemon zest. Cover
with another half pepper and secure as a parcel with string.

Chargrill parcels on medium heat for 3 to 5 minutes each side,
until cheese begins to melt. Spoon some lemon juice over
peppers and serve immediately.

Cook's note Soak kitchen string in water for 20 minutes
before using so it doesn't burn on the barbecue.

EGGPLANT ROTOLO

Serves 4

3 Tbsp olive oil

1 large eggplant
(aubergine), thinly sliced
lengthwise

12 large slices chargrilled
bell pepper (capiscum)

4 bocconcini, thinly sliced

12 large basil leaves

12 cocktail picks

arugula (rocket),
for serving

Preheat oven to 400ºF (200ºC).

Heat oil in a skillet (fry-pan) on high heat. Fry eggplant in batches, turning once, until golden brown and tender. Drain on paper towels.

Lay slices of eggplant flat. Place 1 piece of chargrilled pepper, 1 bocconcini slice and 1 basil leaf on each piece. Roll up and secure with a cocktail pick.

Place in a roasting pan and bake for 10 minutes. Serve with a few arugula leaves.

FENNEL, BEET & ORANGE SALAD

Serves 4

2 oranges, peeled

15oz (450g) can baby beets, drained

1 small fennel bulb, halved and finely sliced

6oz (150g) feta, crumbled

5 tsp extra virgin olive oil

2 tsp red wine vinegar

¼ tsp salt

freshly ground black pepper

2 tsp dill sprigs

Use a small, sharp knife to remove any white pith from oranges, then cut fruit into segments. Cut beets in half.

Arrange fennel, orange and beets on serving plates and sprinkle with crumbled feta.

Whisk together oil, vinegar, salt and a good grinding of pepper. Spoon over salads. Scatter dill over salads and serve.

ASIAN CUCUMBER & CABBAGE SALAD

Serves 4

1 long cucumber

7oz (200g) firm tofu, drained and cut in ½ inch (1.2 cm) cubes

½ Napa cabbage (wong bok), finely shredded

1½ cups (120g) mung bean sprouts

6 scallions (spring onions), thinly sliced

¼ cup (10g) cilantro (coriander) sprigs

Dressing

4 tsp finely grated fresh ginger

¼ cup (60ml) peanut oil

3 Tbsp light soy sauce

3 Tbsp rice vinegar

2 tsp sesame oil

1 Tbsp toasted sesame seeds

1 tsp salt

freshly ground black pepper

Use a vegetable peeler to slice cucumber into ribbons. Place in a serving bowl with tofu, cabbage, sprouts and scallion.

To make dressing, whisk all ingredients together in a small bowl.

Pour dressing over salad and toss well. Scatter cilantro over salad before serving.

STEAMED TOFU WITH CILANTRO

Serves 4

6 scallions (spring onions), cut in matchsticks

2 inch (5 cm) piece of fresh ginger, cut in matchsticks

¾ cup (25g) cilantro (coriander) leaves

1lb 5oz (600g) silken tofu, sliced

⅓ cup (80ml) light soy sauce

3 Tbsp peanut oil

2 tsp sesame oil

Combine scallion, ginger and cilantro in a mixing bowl. Use half this mixture to line bases of 4 small, shallow bowls.

Divide tofu among bowls, arranging it on the greens, then place bowls in a steamer basket. Cover and steam over a pan or wok of boiling water for 5 minutes, until heated through.

Top tofu with remaining greens. Sprinkle with soy sauce.

Heat oils in a small saucepan. Pour oils over tofu and serve immediately.

STUFFED TOMATOES

Makes 8

¾ cup (135g) instant couscous

¾ cup (190ml) boiling water

4 tsp olive oil

4oz (100g) small white mushrooms, sliced

1 clove garlic, crushed

½ tsp salt

1 tsp ras el hanout (Moroccan seasoning: see glossary, page 309)

¼ tsp chili powder

1 cup (30g) baby spinach leaves

4oz (100g) ricotta

⅓ cup (50g) sliced pitted black olives

¼ cup (10g) torn mint leaves

8 medium-sized tomatoes

Preheat oven to 350°F (180°C). Lightly grease and line a roasting pan with parchment paper.

In a heatproof bowl, combine couscous and water, stirring once to mix. Cover immediately and set aside for 5 minutes. Fluff couscous with a fork.

Meanwhile, heat oil in a skillet (fry-pan) on medium-high heat. Sauté mushroom and garlic for 3 to 4 minutes, until tender. Add salt, ras el hanout and chili powder. Cook for 1 minute. Stir in spinach, and cook for 1 to 2 minutes, until spinach wilts.

Add mushroom mixture to couscous with ricotta, olives and mint. Stir gently to combine.

Slice top from each tomato and scoop out flesh using a teaspoon or melon baller. Spoon couscous mixture into tomato cases and arrange closely together in prepared pan. Place lids on top of tomatoes.

Bake for 15 to 20 minutes, until tomatoes are tender and beginning to collapse. Spoon carefully onto serving plates while still warm.

ZUCCHINI FRITTERS WITH TZATZIKI

Makes 32 small fritters

1lb (450g) zucchini (courgettes), coarsely grated

olive oil, for cooking

1 onion, finely chopped

2 scallions (spring onions), finely chopped

1 clove garlic, crushed

4 eggs, beaten

7oz (200g) feta, crumbled

1 ½ cups (90g) soft fresh breadcrumbs

¼ cup (35g) all-purpose (plain) flour

¼ cup (25g) grated parmesan

2 Tbsp each chopped dill and oregano

½ tsp salt

freshly ground black pepper

Tzatziki

¼ long cucumber, deseeded and coarsely grated

2 cloves garlic, crushed

2 Tbsp chopped fresh mint

1 cup (225g) thick, unsweetened Greek-style yogurt

Squeeze as much liquid as possible from the grated zucchini, then place zucchini in a bowl.

Heat 3 Tbsp oil in a skillet (fry-pan) to medium heat, add onion and scallion, then cook for 5 to 10 minutes, until softened but not colored. Add the garlic and cook for 1 minute more. Add this mixture to the bowl containing zucchini.

Stir in eggs, feta, breadcrumbs, flour, parmesan and herbs. Season with salt and pepper and mix well to combine.

Scoop mixture into small fritters and fry in the hot skillet until golden brown on both sides, adding more oil to the pan as necessary. Drain fritters on paper towels.

To make tzatziki, squeeze as much liquid from the cucumber as possible. Combine the cucumber with remaining ingredients, a pinch of salt and 1 Tbsp olive oil. Cover and chill, if making in advance.

Serve fritters hot with tzatziki on the side, for dipping.

Cook's note Authentic Greek yogurt is thick because it is strained. To thicken plain yogurt, place a generous amount in a colander lined with large piece of clean cheesecloth (muslin), place over a bowl and leave in the fridge to drain overnight.

SWISS CHARD & CHEESE PASTRIES

Makes 8

2 Tbsp (30g) butter

1 onion, finely chopped

2 cups (130g) shredded swiss chard (silverbeet)

15oz (420g) artichoke hearts from a jar, drained and chopped

6oz (150g) ricotta

4oz (100g) feta, crumbled

2 eggs, beaten

½ tsp salt

freshly ground black pepper

2 sheets readymade puff pastry, each cut into 4 squares

Tomato salad

2 large tomatoes, sliced

¼ cup (10g) loosely packed basil leaves

1 Tbsp extra virgin olive oil

2 tsp balsamic vinegar

¼ tsp salt

Preheat oven to 400ºF (200ºC). Line a baking sheet with parchment paper.

Melt butter in a skillet (fry-pan) on medium. Sauté onion for 2 to 3 minutes, until soft.

Increase heat to high. Add swiss chard and artichokes. Cook for 3 to 5 minutes, stirring, until greens wilt and liquid evaporates. Transfer to a large bowl to cool.

Mix in ricotta, feta and half the beaten egg. Season with salt and pepper.

Spoon mixture onto one half of each piece of pastry. Brush edges with a little of remaining egg and fold over to enclose filling. Press edges with a fork to seal.

Place pastries on prepared sheet. Brush with egg. Make a few small air vent slits in the top of each. Bake 15 to 20 minutes, until golden.

Meanwhile, to make tomato salad, combine all the ingredients.

Serve pastries hot, with tomato salad.

RED ONION TARTLETS WITH BLUE CHEESE

Makes 6

8 small red onions, peeled and cut into wedges

1 Tbsp olive oil

1 tsp salt

freshly ground black pepper

2 sheets readymade puff pastry

1 egg

1 Tbsp milk

1 Tbsp thyme leaves

5oz (150g) blue cheese, cut in 6 wedges

Preheat oven to 425°F (220°C). Line two baking sheets with parchment paper.

Place onion wedges in a small roasting pan, drizzle with olive oil and season with salt and pepper. Roast for 10 minutes, stirring once during cooking. Remove from the oven and allow to cool a little.

Use a 5 inch (12 cm) round cutter to cut three circles from each pastry sheet. Place circles on prepared sheets. Whisk egg and milk together and brush onto pastry to glaze.

Arrange a small mound of onion wedges in the center of each pastry circle, leaving the edges free of topping so the pastry can puff when cooked.

Bake for 15 to 20 minutes, or until pastry edges are puffed and golden brown. Immediately top each tartet with a wedge of blue cheese and thyme leaves, and serve warm.

GNOCCHI,
NOODLES,
RISOTTO

COOKING CLASS | POTATO GNOCCHI

POTATO GNOCCHI

Serves 6

2lb (1kg) waxy potatoes such as Red Rose or Yukon Gold, whole, unpeeled

1¼ cups (160g) all-purpose (plain) flour + ½ cup (65g) extra

1 tsp salt

2 egg yolks

Burnt sage butter

6 Tbsp (100g) butter

1 clove garlic, crushed

4 tsp chopped sage leaves + extra whole leaves

shaved parmesan, for serving

Boil whole potatoes in just enough water to cover for 15 minutes, or until tender. Drain well, cool a little, then peel and push through a ricer, or mash. Gently stir in 1¼ cups (160g) flour, the salt and egg yolks. As dough stiffens, turn out onto floured work surface.

Knead mixture for a few minutes until a soft, elastic dough forms, using extra flour to help

164

prevent sticking. Scrape up any dough that sticks to the work surface.

Form dough into fourths. Using flour to dust your hands and work surface, knead each piece of dough lightly, and roll into a long, ½ inch-diameter (1.2 cm) log. Cut into 1 inch (2.5 cm) pieces. Press each piece gently around your finger to put a curve into it, then press with a fork to make ribbed grooves.

Drop gnocchi, in batches, into a large saucepan of boiling, salted water. After a few minutes, the pieces will float to the surface. Cook 1 more minute. Remove with a slotted spoon.

To make burnt sage butter, melt butter in a small saucepan with garlic and chopped sage. Cook until butter begins to turn golden brown. Remove from heat and toss with cooked hot gnocchi. Fry extra sage leaves to garnish. Serve gnocchi with shaved parmesan.

Cook's note This traditional way to shape gnocchi is not just decorative — it helps the gnocchi cook evenly, and the grooves trap the sauce.

BEET RAVIOLI WITH OREGANO

Serves 6

1lb 6oz (625g) medium beets, ends trimmed

2 large cloves garlic, unpeeled

2 tsp fresh oregano leaves + sprigs, for serving

6 Tbsp (100g) unsalted butter, softened

48 readymade round wonton wrappers

1 egg, lightly beaten

Preheat oven to 350°F (180°C).

Place beets, garlic and oregano on a large piece of aluminum foil. Enclose and seal. Place package on a baking sheet and bake for 50 minutes, until beets are tender. Unwrap and set aside just until cool enough to handle.

Rub skin from beets and peel garlic. Transfer beets, garlic and oregano to a food processor with 2 Tbsp of butter and process until smooth. Season to taste.

Lay half of the wrappers on a floured work surface. Place 2 teaspoons of beet mixture in center of each wrapper. Brush edges with egg. Cover each with another wrapper, to enclose filling. Press edges to seal, ensuring air is expelled.

Cook ravioli, a few at a time, in a large saucepan of simmering, salted water for 3 minutes, or until they rise to the surface. Transfer cooked ravioli to warm bowls.

Melt remaining butter in a small pan on low heat for 2 minutes, or until butter turns a nut-brown color. Spoon brown butter over ravioli and sprinkle with oregano sprigs. Serve immediately.

SOBA NOODLE & VEGETABLE SALAD

Serves 4

2 red bell peppers (capsicums), halved and deseeded

16 green beans, trimmed and halved

5oz (150g) snow peas (mangetouts), halved

10 asparagus spears, each cut in two

12oz (360g) dried soba noodles

10oz (300g) firm tofu, cut in cubes

1 cup (40g) crispy egg noodles

Dressing

1 clove garlic, crushed

1 tsp prepared wasabi paste

¼ cup (60ml) mirin (see glossary, page 307)

3 Tbsp sesame oil

1 tsp finely grated fresh ginger

1 Tbsp vegetable oil

½ tsp salt

freshly ground black pepper

Preheat oven to 400°F (200°C).

Place peppers in a roasting pan. Bake for 20 minutes, or until skins blister. Place peppers in a bowl and cover with plastic wrap. When cool enough to handle, peel peppers and cut them into slices.

Cook beans, snow peas and asparagus in plenty of boiling water for 4 minutes. Drain well and refresh under cold running water.

Cook soba noodles according to packet directions. In the meantime, heat a little oil in a skillet (fry-pan) and quickly cook tofu until golden.

Meanwhile, to make dressing, place all ingredients in a screw-topped jar and shake well to combine.

Gently toss soba noodles, tofu and vegetables together with dressing. Pile salad onto serving plates and scatter crispy noodles over the top.

VEGETABLE BAVETTE WITH PINE NUTS

Serves 4

2 medium zucchini (courgettes), cut into long, thin strips

12oz (350g) dried bavette (or fettucine)

1 Tbsp (15g) butter

6 semi-dried tomatoes, sliced thinly

⅓ cup (40g) pine nuts, toasted

2 scallions (spring onions), thinly sliced

3 Tbsp chopped parsley

3 Tbsp chopped mint

1 Tbsp snipped chives

1 Tbsp extra virgin olive oil

salt and freshly ground black pepper

Blanch zucchini in a large saucepan of boiling, salted water for 30 seconds. Drain and refresh under cold water.

Cook bavette in a large saucepan of boiling, salted water according to packet directions. Drain.

Melt butter in a large skillet (fry-pan) on high heat. Sauté zucchini, tomato, pine nuts and scallion for 1 minute. Add drained bavette, herbs and olive oil. Season to taste and toss over moderate heat to warm through.

Cook's note Bavette are thin flat strips of pasta made without egg. Suitable substitutions include linguine, fettucine or spaghetti.

ORZO SALAD

Serves 4

1lb (450g) eggplant (aubergine), cut in 1 inch (2.5 cm) cubes

2 Tbsp olive oil

salt and freshly ground black pepper

1 ½ cups (300g) dried orzo (risoni) pasta

⅓ cup (10g) chopped parsley

4oz (100g) feta cheese, crumbled

zest and juice of 2 lemons

Preheat oven to 350°F (180°C).

Place eggplant in a large roasting pan, toss with oil, then season with salt and pepper, tossing again. Spread eggplant evenly in the pan and roast for 20 minutes, or until golden brown. Remove to cool.

Meanwhile, cook pasta in plenty of boiling, salted water for 8 minutes, or until just tender to the bite. Drain and rinse under cold water to cool. Drain well and place in a large bowl.

Add cooled eggplant to pasta. Add parsley, feta, lemon zest and juice and toss well to combine.

CRISP NOODLE SALAD WITH GINGER DRESSING

Serves 4

Dressing

2 Tbsp light soy sauce

1 Tbsp sesame oil

1 inch (2.5cm) piece fresh ginger, finely grated

½ cup (15g) chopped cilantro (coriander)

Salad

14oz (425g) can whole baby sweetcorn, drained

8oz (227g) can water chestnuts, drained

1 red bell pepper (capsicum), deseeded and finely sliced

1 cup (80g) mung bean sprouts

4 scallions (spring onions), finely sliced on an angle

5 ½ oz (150g) crispy egg noodles

Make dressing by whisking together soy sauce, sesame oil, ginger and cilantro in a small bowl.

Place all salad ingredients except noodles in a large mixing bowl. Pour dressing over salad and toss gently, but thoroughly, to combine.

Add noodles and toss again briefly. Serve immediately.

FRESH TOMATO, RICOTTA & BASIL PENNE

Serves 4

14oz (400g) dried penne

1 Tbsp extra virgin olive oil

1 clove garlic, crushed

6 medium tomatoes, diced

7oz (200g) ricotta, crumbled

1 cup (30g) torn basil leaves

½ tsp salt

freshly ground black pepper

Cook penne in a large saucepan of boiling, salted water according to packet directions. Drain.

Place hot pasta, oil and garlic in a large bowl. Add remaining ingredients. Toss to combine and serve.

TOMATO, ASPARAGUS & PESTO FETTUCINE

Serves 4

1lb (450g) dried fettucine

2 tsp extra virgin olive oil

¼ cup (60ml) olive oil

7oz (200g) punnet cherry tomatoes, halved

7oz (200g) asparagus, sliced

2 tsp chili paste

2 cloves garlic, crushed

½ cup (125ml) prepared basil pesto (see page 14)

salt and freshly ground black pepper

4oz (100g) chèvre (goat's cheese), crumbled

Cook fettucine in a large saucepan of boiling, salted water, following packet instructions. Drain well, reserving ½ cup (125ml) of cooking water for sauce. Return pasta to pan with extra virgin olive oil to keep warm.

Heat olive oil in a large skillet (fry-pan) on medium-high heat. Sauté tomatoes, asparagus, chili paste and garlic for 2 to 3 minutes, until tomatoes collapse. Toss through hot pasta with pesto and reserved water. Season to taste with salt and pepper. Serve topped with chèvre.

SPINACH & RICOTTA CANNELLONI

Serves 4

1 Tbsp olive oil

1 onion, finely chopped

2 cloves garlic, chopped

11oz (300g) frozen cooked spinach, defrosted

9oz (250g) ricotta (or cottage cheese, if preferred)

1 egg, lightly beaten

1 tsp salt

freshly ground black pepper

5oz (125g) dried cannelloni tubes

1lb 3oz (550g) jar good quality tomato pasta sauce

½ cup (125ml) cream

¼ cup (25g) grated parmesan

Preheat oven to 325°F (170°C). Grease an ovenproof dish. Heat oil in a pan on medium heat. Add onion and cook for 5 minutes to soften. Add garlic and cook for 1 minute more. Transfer mixture to a bowl.

Squeeze as much liquid from the spinach as possible. Add the spinach, ricotta and beaten egg to the onion mixture and stir to combine. Season with salt and pepper.

Spoon prepared mixture into a piping bag fitted with a plain wide nozzle and pipe into the cannelloni tubes, to fill. Place filled cannelloni in prepared dish.

Combine the tomato pasta sauce with the cream and pour over the cannelloni. Sprinkle the surface with grated parmesan and bake for 30 to 40 minutes, or until golden brown and the pasta is tender.

Cook's note Piping the mixture into the cannelloni tubes is the easiest way to fill them, but you can push the mixture into the tubes with a teaspoon, if necessary.

SQUASH, SAGE & TWO CHEESE CANNELLONI

Serves 4

1lb 5oz (600g) butternut squash, peeled and chopped in chunks

7oz (200g) ricotta

2 Tbsp roughly chopped sage

salt and freshly ground black pepper

12 dried cannelloni tubes

14oz (410g) can tomato purée

1 cup (125g) grated cheddar

Preheat oven to 350°F (180°C). Lightly grease a 6 cup (1.5L) ovenproof dish.

Place squash in a large pan of boiling salted water. Cook 5 to 10 minutes, until tender. Drain well and mash. Transfer to a large bowl. Cool.

Beat ricotta and sage into squash and season to taste with salt and pepper. Spoon or pipe into cannelloni tubes.

Pour half the tomato purée into the base of prepared dish and spread to make an even layer. Sprinkle with half the cheddar, and top with a single layer of cannelloni tubes. Top with remaining tomato purée and cheese.

Cover dish with aluminum foil. Bake 30 minutes. Uncover and bake a further 15 to 20 minutes, until cannelloni is tender and cheese lightly browned.

MUSHROOM & SPINACH LASAGNE

Serves 4

4 tsp olive oil

1 onion, finely chopped

2 cloves garlic, crushed

14oz (400g) can diced tomatoes

9oz (250g) small white mushrooms, sliced

1lb 8oz (680g) fresh spinach, trimmed and roughly chopped

salt and freshly ground black pepper

1lb 2oz (500g) fresh ricotta

¾ cup (190ml) milk

2 eggs, lightly beaten

4 readymade fresh lasagne sheets

½ cup (45g) grated parmesan

Preheat oven to 400°F (200°C). Lightly grease a 8 cup (2L) ovenproof lasagne dish.

In a large saucepan, heat half the oil on high heat. Sauté onion and garlic for 2 to 3 minutes, until tender. Stir in tomato. Remove from pan and set aside.

Wipe out pan. Heat remaining oil in pan on high heat. Sauté mushrooms for 2 to 3 minutes, until tender. Add spinach, cook for 1 to 2 minutes, just until spinach wilts. Season to taste with salt and pepper.

In a large bowl, combine ricotta, milk and eggs. Season.

Spoon one third of the tomato mixture into prepared dish. Cover with two lasagne sheets, cutting to fit. Spoon over another third of the tomato mixture, half of the mushroom mixture and half of the ricotta mixture.

Repeat layers, finishing with ricotta mixture. Sprinkle with parmesan. Bake 35 to 40 minutes, until tender and golden. Serve with a salad.

EGG NOODLES WITH GINGER TEMPEH

Serves 4

8oz (225g) dried egg noodles

2 tsp peanut oil

13oz (375g) block tempeh, sliced (see glossary, page 301)

14oz (400g) asparagus, each spear cut in two

2 cloves garlic, crushed

3 Tbsp finely grated ginger

3 scallions (spring onions), sliced

1 cup (80g) mung bean sprouts

¼ cup (60ml) kecap manis (see glossary, page 310)

1 tsp sesame oil

¼ cup (60ml) water

½ cup (15g) cilantro (coriander) sprigs

Cook noodles according to packet directions, until tender but still firm. Drain and rinse under cold running water to stop cooking. Spread out on a clean dish towel for at least 1 hour, until dry.

Heat 1 tsp peanut oil in a wok on medium heat. Cook tempeh slices for 2 minutes each side, until golden. Remove from wok and set aside. Heat remaining oil in wok on high. Stir-fry asparagus, garlic, ginger and scallions for 2 to 3 minutes, until asparagus is bright green. Remove from wok.

Add prepared noodles to wok and stir-fry on very high heat for 4 minutes, until noodles separate and dry out slightly. Add mung bean sprouts and cook for 2 minutes. Combine kecap manis, sesame oil and water in a bowl and stir into noodles in wok. Return asparagus mixture and tempeh to noodles and toss to heat through. Scatter cilantro on top.

VEGETABLE CHOW MEIN

Serves 4

3 Tbsp peanut oil

1 onion, sliced

2 cloves garlic, crushed

1 carrot, halved and sliced

3 Tbsp soy sauce

1 Tbsp sugar

2 tsp ground star anise

1 mild red chili, deseeded and sliced

1 celeryrib, thinly sliced

4oz (100g) snow peas (mangetouts), sliced

½ cup (60g) canned bamboo shoot slices, drained

8oz (225g) packet dried egg noodles, soaked and drained

sliced scallion (spring onion), for serving

Omelet

3 eggs

2 Tbsp toasted sesame seeds

2 tsp sesame oil

Heat half the peanut oil in a wok on high heat. Stir-fry onion and garlic for 1 minute, until onion is soft. Add the carrot and stir-fry for 1 to 2 minutes.

Whisk together soy sauce, sugar and star anise. Set aside.

To make omelet, heat a small, non-stick skillet (fry-pan) on medium heat. Whisk eggs, sesame seeds and oil together, until well-combined. Pour into pan and swirl mixture around to cover base of pan. Cook for 1 to 2 minutes, until the surface starts to set. Loosen the edges with a spatula. Flip edges in towards center to fold into thirds, and remove. Slice into strips and set aside.

Add remaining peanut oil to wok on high heat. Add chili, celery, snow peas and bamboo shoots. Stir-fry for 1 to 2 minutes, until vegetables are tender. Toss noodles and reserved sauce through. Stir-fry for 2 minutes more.

Serve chow mein topped with omelet and scallion.

ROASTED SQUASH RISOTTO

Serves 4

2lb (900g) butternut squash, peeled and diced

2 Tbsp olive oil

salt and freshly ground black pepper

4 cups (1L) vegetable stock

1 onion, chopped

2 garlic cloves, crushed

1 ½ cups (330g) Arborio rice

¼ cup (25g) parmesan, grated

1 Tbsp parsley, chopped

extra chopped parsley, for serving

extra grated parmesan, for serving

Preheat oven to 400°F (200°C). Line a roasting pan with parchment paper.

Toss squash and 1 tablespoon of olive oil in a bowl. Season generously with salt and pepper. Spread in a single layer in the prepared pan. Bake for 20 to 25 minutes, until just tender.

Bring stock to a simmer and keep hot over a low heat. Heat another tablespoon of olive oil in a large heavy-based saucepan over medium heat. Sauté onion and garlic for 3 to 4 minutes, or until the onion softens.

Add Arborio rice and cook, stirring, for 1 to 2 minutes, until the rice grains start to become translucent.

Add 1 cup (250ml) of the hot stock to the rice, stirring often, until the rice absorbs the liquid. Continue stirring in stock, 1 cup at a time, allowing each to be absorbed before adding the next. Stir until rice is just tender and creamy, about 20 minutes.

Add squash, grated parmesan and chopped parsley to risotto. Season to taste. Serve topped with extra chopped parsley and grated parmesan.

LEMON & ASPARAGUS BARLEY RISOTTO

Serves 4

2 tsp olive oil

1 red onion, finely chopped

1 ½ cups (315g) pearl barley

5 cups (1.25L) vegetable stock

7oz (200g) asparagus, each spear cut into 3

1 red bell pepper (capsicum), chargrilled, peeled and deseeded

juice and finely grated zest of 1 lemon

4 eggs

¼ cup (25g) grated parmesan

Heat stock in a saucepan and reduce heat to low.

Heat oil in a heavy-based saucepan on medium. Sauté onion for 2 to 3 minutes, until starting to color. Stir in barley and cook for 2 minutes, until toasted.

Add stock, one ladle at time, stirring after each addition, until absorbed and barley is just tender, about 20 minutes. Add asparagus, capsicum and lemon with the last of the stock.

Poach the eggs in simmering water until the yolks are soft-cooked.

Use a fork to separate grains of risotto, then serve in bowls, and top each with a poached egg and some parmesan.

ENTRÉES

ENTERTAINING MENU
FALL HARVEST FEAST

Celebrate the rich flavors and colors of fall with a lavish feast for friends and family.

Set a themed table with candles for a golden, warm glow. Cut some branches of burnished leaves for a vase, or gather just a few leaves and chestnuts to scatter on the table. Polish your best dinner service and enjoy the warmth of indoors.

Serve the entrée buffet-style on warm platters in the center of the table so your guests can pick and choose to create their ultimate feast.

Snacks
- Potato and garlic dip
- Spiced nuts

Soup
- Roasted carrot and parsnip soup

Entrées
- Roasted pumpkin risotto
- Roasted chili garlic eggplant
- Roasted white onions with blue cheese

Side
- Garden salad with walnuts

The cooler months are ideal for indulging in rich desserts. Celebrate the fall harvest with some home baking — apple pie, chocolate pecan tart or spiced pear cake would be ideal.

RED CURRY, STIR-FRIED BEANS & TOFU

Serves 4

2 Tbsp peanut oil

2 large onions, roughly chopped

12oz (350g) firm tofu, drained and cut into 1 inch (2.5cm) cubes

2 Tbsp Thai red curry paste

14oz (410g) can chopped tomatoes

11oz (300g) green beans, trimmed and halved crosswise

Heat the oil in a wok on high heat, add the onion and cubed tofu, then stir-fry for 3 to 5 minutes, until golden brown. Remove onion and tofu and set aside.

Add curry paste to the wok and stir-fry 1 minute. Stir in the tomatoes and bring to a boil. Add the green beans and return tofu and onion to the pan.

Simmer for 5 minutes, remove from the heat and serve.

ASPARAGUS & GRUYÈRE TART

Serves 4

1 ½ cups (190g)
all-purpose (plain) flour

1 stick (125g) cold butter,
chopped

1 egg yolk

about 2 Tbsp iced water

Filling
10 asparagus spears,
trimmed and halved

8 ½ oz (250g) frozen
spinach, defrosted and
squeezed dry

2 eggs

½ cup (125ml) heavy
(double) cream

¼ cup (60ml) milk

½ tsp salt

freshly ground black pepper

⅔ cup (80g) grated gruyère

Sift flour into a large bowl. Add butter. Rub in, using fingertips, until mixture resembles breadcrumbs. Add egg yolk and enough water to make a firm but pliable dough. Knead lightly.

Wrap dough in plastic wrap and refrigerate for 30 minutes.

Preheat oven to 400°F (200°C). Lightly grease a 14 x 5 inch (35 x 12.5 cm) loose-bottomed rectangular flan pan. Place on a baking sheet.

Roll pastry into a rectangle between two sheets of parchment paper. Ease into prepared pan. Trim edges. Refrigerate for 15 minutes.

Blind bake pastry (line with paper and fill with rice or ceramic baking weights) for 10 minutes. Remove paper and filling. Bake for a further 5 minutes. Set flan case aside on a rack.

Reduce oven to 350°F (180°C).

To make the filling, whisk together eggs, cream and milk. Season with salt and pepper. Stir in gruyère.

Arrange asparagus and spinach in pastry case and pour over filling mixture. Bake for 35 to 40 minutes, until set. Cool slightly before serving.

LENTIL, BEET & FETA SALAD

Serves 4

12 small beets, ends trimmed

1 Tbsp olive oil

2 cups (60g) loosely packed baby spinach leaves

14oz (410g) can lentils, rinsed and drained

2oz (50g) feta, crumbled

¼ cup (30g) walnuts, toasted and roughly chopped

Dressing

2 Tbsp extra virgin olive oil

1 Tbsp balsamic vinegar

¼ tsp salt

Preheat oven to 400°F (200°C).

Place beets in a roasting pan and toss with oil to coat. Roast for 45 minutes to 1 hour, until tender when tested with a skewer. Cool and cut beets in half.

To make dressing, whisk together oil, vinegar and salt.

Arrange spinach, beets and lentils in a serving dish. Scatter feta and walnuts on top, Spoon dressing over salad and serve.

CELERIAC & POTATO CAKES WITH POACHED EGGS

Serves 4

1lb (450g) celeriac, peeled and coarsely grated

1lb (450g) Desiree potatoes (or other all purpose potatoes), peeled, coarsely grated

1 Tbsp Dijon mustard

1 tsp salt

freshly ground black pepper

1 Tbsp extra virgin olive oil

1 Tbsp unsalted butter

dash of white vinegar, for poaching eggs

4 eggs

¼ cup (10g) celery leaves

Combine celeriac, potato and mustard in a large mixing bowl. Season with salt and pepper. Toss lightly to mix using hands.

Heat oil and butter in a non-stick skillet (fry-pan) on medium heat, until butter melts. Drop ¼ cup measures of celeriac mixture into pan, pressing down to form cakes, leaving 1 inch (2.5 cm) space between them. Cook for 3 to 4 minutes each side, until golden and crisp.

Meanwhile, half-fill a saucepan with salted water and a dash of vinegar and heat until simmering. Poach the eggs in the simmering water until the yolks are soft and still runny. Remove eggs using a slotted spoon, and drain off any water.

Serve celeriac and potato cakes topped with poached egg, and scatter celery leaves on top.

SALT & PEPPER TOFU

Serves 4

¼ cup (35g) all-purpose (plain) flour

2 tsp sea salt

1 tsp dried chili flakes

½ tsp freshly ground black pepper

1lb (450g) firm tofu, drained and cut in 1 inch (2.5cm) cubes

⅓ cup (80ml) peanut oil

4 cloves garlic, finely sliced

½ cup (75g) unsalted natural cashews

9oz (250g) choy sum

4 yellow summer squash, cut into wedges

steamed rice, for serving

2 Tbsp soy sauce, for serving

Combine flour, salt, chili flakes and pepper in a bowl. Pat tofu dry on paper towels, add to bowl and carefully toss to coat in seasoned flour.

Heat ¼ cup (60ml) of the oil in a wok on high heat. Cook tofu in batches for 5 minutes, turning, until golden. Drain on paper towels.

Wipe wok clean. Heat remaining oil on medium heat. Stir-fry garlic and cashews for 2 to 3 minutes, until colored. Add vegetables and cook for 3 to 5 minutes, until tender. Stir in tofu. Serve on steamed rice, with soy sauce.

BAKED EGGPLANT, TOMATO & BASIL STACKS

Serves 4

2 eggplants (aubergines) each cut crosswise into 8 slices

2 tsp salt

2 zucchini (courgettes), sliced diagonally

¼ cup (60ml) olive oil + extra for serving

¼ cup (60ml) balsamic vinegar + extra for serving

2 cloves garlic, crushed

4 tomatoes, each cut into 4 thick slices

2 Tbsp light brown (soft brown) sugar

16 slices fresh mozzarella

16 large basil leaves

Preheat oven to 400°F (200°C). Line a baking sheet with parchment paper.

Place eggplant in a bowl and toss with salt. Set aside for 10 minutes. Rinse eggplant and pat dry.

Arrange eggplant and zucchini in a large roasting pan. Whisk together olive oil, balsamic vinegar and garlic, and pour over vegetables, tossing well to coat. Bake for 20 minutes, until tender, turning once.

Arrange sliced tomatoes in a shallow dish and sprinkle with sugar. Cover and set aside for 10 minutes.

Set tomato tops to one side. Starting with largest slices at the bottom, stack eggplant, zucchini, tomato, mozzarella slices and basil leaves in four stacks on prepared sheet. Finish each stack with a tomato top.

Bake for 5 to 10 minutes, until the cheese begins to melt. Serve with a little more olive oil and balsamic vinegar.

BUTTERMILK CORN FLAPJACKS

Makes 10

2 cups (250g) all-purpose (plain) flour

2 ½ tsp baking soda (bicarbonate of soda)

1 ½ cups (375ml) buttermilk

4 eggs, beaten

2 cups (370g) sweetcorn kernels (fresh, or defrosted from frozen)

4oz (100g) feta cheese, crumbed

1 Tbsp chopped fresh sage

salt and freshly ground black pepper

olive oil, for cooking

1lb (450g) baby spinach leaves, washed + extra for serving

1 clove garlic, sliced

¾ cup (190ml) readymade tomato relish, for serving

1 red bell pepper (capsicum), deseeded and cut in thin strips, for serving

Sift flour and baking soda into a mixing bowl and make a well in the center. Pour in the buttermilk and then pour the eggs into the well.

Add the corn, feta and sage and stir to make a batter. Season well with salt and pepper.

Heat 2 tsp olive oil in a non-stick skillet (fry-pan) over a medium heat and, working in batches, fry large ladles of the batter, for 3 to 4 minutes, until browned on the underside.

Flip each flapjack over and brown the other side for 2 to 3 minutes. Remove the cooked flapjacks and set on a baking sheet lined with paper towels. Flapjacks can be kept warm for up to 15 minutes in a 325ºF (160ºC) oven.

Wipe skillet clean and heat another 2 tsp of oil over a high heat. Add spinach and garlic and sauté briefly, until spinach leaves have wilted. Layer flapjacks with spinach and some relish on warm serving plates. Top with some extra spinach leaves and strips of pepper. Serve immediately.

213

BAKED SQUASH WITH BASIL & FETA

Serves 4

½ kabochah squash (Japanese pumpkin), deseeded, skin on, cut into 8 wedges

1 Tbsp olive oil

salt and freshly ground black pepper

7oz (200g) chargrilled peppers (capsicum), roughly chopped

⅔ cup (40g) soft fresh breadcrumbs

4oz (100g) feta, crumbled

2 tomatoes, deseeded and diced

¼ cup (30g) pine nuts

¼ cup (10g) roughly chopped basil + extra, for serving

1 clove garlic, crushed

Preheat oven to 400°F (200°C). Line a roasting pan with parchment paper.

Arrange squash, skin-side down, on prepared tray and brush flesh with oil. Season with salt and pepper. Bake for 20 minutes, or until just tender.

Meanwhile, in a large bowl, combine chargrilled pepper, breadcrumbs, feta, tomato, pine nuts, basil and garlic. Mix well and season.

Lay squash wedges flat in pan. Spoon an even amount of feta mixture onto each wedge. Bake for 10 to 15 minutes, until golden. Scatter extra basil leaves on top.

BEAN ENCHILADAS

Serves 6

1 Tbsp olive oil

1 onion, finely chopped

3 cloves garlic, crushed

2 tsp cumin

2 x 14oz (410g) cans kidney beans, rinsed and drained

1 cup (250ml) tomato pasta sauce + ½ cup (125ml) extra

½ tsp chili powder

¼ cup (10g) chopped cilantro (coriander)

salt and freshly ground black pepper

6 large flour tortillas

1 cup (125g) grated cheddar

Preheat oven to 350°F (180°C). Grease an ovenproof dish.

Heat oil in a saucepan over a medium heat and cook onion for 5 minutes, until soft. Add garlic and cumin and cook for 1 minute more.

Add a can of kidney beans to saucepan. Roughly mash the second can of beans and add to the pan. Stir in 1 cup (250ml) tomato pasta sauce, the chili powder and cilantro.

Simmer on low heat for 2 minutes, or until heated through. Season with salt and pepper, to taste.

Fill each tortilla with one sixth of the bean mixture and roll up, leaving ends open.

Arrange enchiladas, seam-side down, in prepared dish. Spread with extra tomato pasta sauce and sprinkle with grated cheese. Bake for 20 minutes, or until golden brown on top.

BARLEY HOTPOT

Serves 4

1 cup (210g) pearl barley

4 cups (1L) chicken stock

3 cups (750ml) water

2 tsp olive oil

2 onions, finely chopped

2 carrots, peeled and diced small

2 zucchini (courgettes), cut into small dice

1 red bell pepper (capsicum), cut into small dice

2 cloves garlic, crushed

salt and freshly ground black pepper

¼ cup (10g) chopped parsley

½ cup (45g) shaved parmesan, for serving

Place barley in a large saucepan and cover with stock and water. Bring to a boil, cover and reduce heat to low. Simmer for 30 minutes, until tender. Drain, reserving 1 cup (250ml) of cooking liquid, and set aside.

Meanwhile, heat the olive oil in a skillet (fry-pan) on medium heat. Sauté onion and carrot for 5 minutes, until tender. Add the zucchini, pepper and garlic and cook, covered, for another 6 minutes. Stir in the barley, add just enough of the reserved liquid to moisten, season to taste and heat through for 2 minutes.

Stir parsley into barley and vegetables. Serve topped with shaved parmesan.

FRIED BROWN RICE WITH OMELET

Serves 4

2 tsp peanut oil

3 eggs, lightly beaten

1 red bell pepper (capsicum), deseeded and diced

9oz (250g) bunch broccolini, roughly chopped

5oz (150g) small white mushrooms, sliced

9oz (250g) choy sum, roughly chopped

2 ½ cups (475g) cooked brown rice

3 Tbsp Thai sweet chili sauce

4 tsp hoisin sauce

4 tsp soy sauce

1 tsp sesame oil

sliced jalapeño, for serving

sliced scallions (spring onions), for serving

Heat 1 tsp oil in a wok or large skillet (fry-pan) on high heat. Add eggs, swirling to cover base. Cook for 1 to 2 minutes, until just set. Turn and cook for 1 minute. Remove from wok and roll up tightly. Slice thinly.

Heat 1 tsp oil in wok. Stir-fry pepper and broccolini for 2 minutes, until tender. Add mushrooms and choy sum, and stir-fry for 1 minute.

Add rice to wok with all the sauces and the sesame oil. Stir-fry for 1 to 2 minutes, until heated through. Serve topped with omelet, chili and scallions.

CHÈVRE, HAZELNUT & QUINOA SALAD

Serves 4

1 ½ cups (255g) quinoa, rinsed and drained

3 cups (750ml) water

¼ cup (30g) finely chopped natural hazelnuts

¼ cup (30g) finely chopped pecans

3 ½ oz (100g) chèvre (goat's cheese)

3oz (80g) baby arugula (rocket)

1 cup (300g) canned kidney beans, rinsed and drained

9oz (250g) baby plum (roma) or yellow pear tomatoes, halved

1 long cucumber, diced

⅓ cup (55g) currants

2 Tbsp vegetable oil

¼ cup (20g) chickpea sprouts (or other sprouts)

½ cup (15g) mint leaves

Dressing

¼ cup (60ml) olive oil

1 Tbsp lemon juice

2 tsp white wine vinegar

1 tsp sugar

½ tsp dried oregano

salt

Combine quinoa and water in a large saucepan. Bring to a boil on high heat and cook for 5 minutes. Reduce heat to low and simmer, covered, for 15 minutes, until grains are tender. Set aside for 5 minutes. Fluff with a fork and transfer to a large mixing bowl.

In another bowl, combine nuts. Roll heaped teaspoons of chèvre into patties, flatten, then dip into nuts to coat. Refrigerate for at least 30 minutes, until firm.

To make the dressing, whisk all ingredients together and season to taste with salt.

Add arugula, kidney beans, tomatoes, cucumber and currants to quinoa. Toss to combine and pile onto serving plates.

Heat vegetable oil in a small skillet (fry-pan) on medium heat. Fry chèvre patties for a few seconds each side until golden. Drain on paper towels and add to salads. Scatter sprouts and mint over salads, then spoon dressing over the top.

GRILLED SPINACH CHEESE PARCELS

Serves 6

¼ cup (60ml) vegetable oil

1 onion, finely chopped

1lb (450g) spinach, washed and chopped

7oz (200g) feta, crumbled

½ cup (15g) chopped parsley

salt and freshly ground black pepper

2 cups (250g) all-purpose (plain) flour + extra, for dusting

¾ cup (190ml) warm water

Preheat grill plate to low heat.

In a large skillet (fry-pan), heat 1 tablespoon oil on medium heat. Sauté onion for 3 minutes, until soft. Remove onion and set aside. Cook spinach in same pan for 2 minutes, until wilted. Combine onion, spinach, feta and parsley in a mixing bowl. Season with salt and pepper and allow to cool.

Combine flour with a pinch of salt in a mixing bowl. Gradually stir in warm water, until a soft dough forms, adding more water, if necessary. Knead on lightly floured work surface until elastic and smooth.

Divide dough into three equal pieces. Roll out each piece between two sheets of parchment paper into a 10 inch (25 cm) round. Peel away top layer of paper.

Divide spinach filling among rounds of dough, then fold each one in half. Fold in edges to form a rectangle, pinching them to seal.

Lightly oil grill plate. Carefully transfer parcels to it and cook for 3 minutes each side, brushing with oil and turning, using metal spatulas, until golden and crisp. Cut each parcel in half and serve immediately.

THAI GREEN VEGETABLE CURRY

Serves 4

1 Tbsp peanut oil

1 red onion, sliced

⅓ cup (100g) Thai green curry paste

1 long green chili, crushed with the flat side of a knife blade

2 kaffir lime leaves (makrut), slightly crushed (see glossary, page 307)

1 cinnamon stick

1 cup (250ml) vegetable stock

1lb 5oz (600g) sweet potato, peeled and diced

1¼ cups (125g) small cauliflower florets

1 chayote (choko), peeled, deseeded and cut in wedges (optional)

14oz (410g) can coconut milk

4 tsp light brown (soft brown) sugar

4 Tbsp unsalted roasted peanuts, for serving

½ cup (15g) cilantro (coriander) leaves, for serving

steamed rice, for serving

Cucumber salad

¼ cup (60ml) lime juice

2 tsp superfine (caster) sugar

1 long cucumber, diced

1 cup (165g) diced fresh pineapple

¼ cup (25g) unsweetened shredded coconut, toasted

¼ cup (10g) torn mint leaves

Heat oil in a large skillet (fry-pan) on medium-high heat. Sauté onion for 1 to 2 minutes, until soft. Add curry paste and cook, stirring, for 1 to 2 minutes, until aromatic. Add chili, kaffir lime leaves and cinnamon stick.

Stir in stock and bring to a boil. Add sweet potato and reduce heat to low. Simmer, covered, for 10 minutes, until sweet potato is just tender.

Mix cauliflower and chayote into curry. Blend in coconut milk and brown sugar. Simmer, uncovered, for 10 to 12 minutes, until all vegetables are tender.

Meanwhile, to make cucumber salad, stir lime juice and sugar together in a medium-sized bowl. Add cucumber, pineapple, half the coconut and all the mint. Toss gently to combine. Spoon into serving bowls and top with remaining coconut. Serve salad as a side dish to the curry.

SQUASH, HALOUMI & ARUGULA SALAD

Serves 4

2 Tbsp olive oil

½ tsp piri piri seasoning (see glossary, page 309), or dried chili flakes

13oz (360g) haloumi, cut in ¼ inch (6mm) slices

1lb (450g) butternut squash, peeled and cut in ½ inch (1.2 cm) slices

9oz (250g) arugula (rocket)

¼ cup (30g) walnuts, roughly chopped and toasted

Dressing

3 Tbsp white wine vinegar

1 Tbsp Dijon mustard

⅓ cup (80ml) extra virgin olive oil

salt and freshly ground black pepper

Preheat a chargrill to high heat.

Combine 1 Tbsp olive oil and piri piri in a bowl. Add haloumi and turn to coat cheese well.

Brush squash with remaining olive oil. Grill squash for 3 to 5 minutes each side, until tender. Cook haloumi for 2 minutes each side, until grill marks appear.

To make the dressing, combine vinegar and mustard in a bowl. Gradually whisk in the oil. Season to taste with salt and pepper.

Toss arugula and dressing. Arrange squash, haloumi and walnuts on serving plates and top with arugula.

POACHED EGGS, ASPARAGUS & SOFT POLENTA

Serves 4

3 cups (750ml) water

salt

1 cup (170g) instant polenta

½ cup (45g) grated parmesan

1 tsp white vinegar

4 eggs

2 Tbsp (30g) butter

2 bunches asparagus, trimmed

2 cloves garlic, crushed

freshly ground black pepper

Bring water with 1 tsp salt to a boil in a heavy-based saucepan on high heat. Pour in polenta and stir until boiling. Reduce heat to low and cook for 5 minutes, stirring often, until thick. Remove from heat, stir in parmesan, cover and keep warm.

Bring a large saucepan half-filled with water to a boil, then reduce heat to a simmer. Add vinegar and a pinch of salt. One by one, break eggs into a cup and slide them into the bubbling water. Cover with a lid and turn off heat. Leave for 3 minutes. Lift eggs out using a slotted spoon. Drain.

Meanwhile, cook asparagus for 1 minute in boiling water, then drain and refresh under cold running water. Drain again.

Melt butter in a skillet (fry-pan) on medium heat. Add asparagus and garlic and stir-fry for 1 minute, until garlic is soft and golden.

Spoon polenta onto warm plates. Top with asparagus, a poached egg and a grinding of pepper. Spoon garlic butter from the skillet over the top.

RAW ENERGY SALAD

Serves 4

1 small iceberg lettuce

1 large beet, peeled and coarsely grated

3 large carrots, peeled and coarsely grated

½ cup (75g) natural walnut pieces

½ cup (65g) sunflower seeds

3 Tbsp sesame seeds

Dressing

juice of 1 lemon

¼ cup (60ml) extra virgin avocado oil or extra virgin olive oil

salt and freshly ground black pepper

Separate lettuce leaves, setting aside four large leaves to use as cups. Shred remaining leaves. Arrange shredded lettuce inside whole leaves. Top with grated beet and carrot, then sprinkle with nuts and seeds.

Place dressing ingredients in a small bowl and whisk to combine, seasoning to taste with salt and pepper. Pour dressing over salad just before serving.

Cook's note Extra virgin avocado oil is available from specialist food stores, and from online retailers.

PUMPKIN, SPINACH & CHICKPEA CURRY

Serves 4

1 Tbsp vegetable oil

1 onion, sliced

¼ cup (75g) mild Indian curry paste

2lb (900g) blue hubbard squash (crown prince pumpkin), peeled, cut into 1 inch (2.5cm) cubes

1 cup (250ml) vegetable stock

14oz (410g) can chickpeas, rinsed and drained

1 cup (250ml) water

7oz (200g) baby spinach leaves

¼ cup (10g) chopped cilantro (coriander) leaves

steamed rice, for serving

Heat oil in a large saucepan over medium heat. Cook onion for 5 minutes, stirring, until soft. Add curry paste and stir for 1 minute, until fragrant.

Add squash and stir to coat. Add stock, chickpeas and water. Bring to a boil, then lower heat, cover, and simmer for 15 minutes, until squash is tender.

Add baby spinach and simmer for 1 minute, until just wilted. Stir through cilantro and serve with steamed rice.

SPINACH & CORN CRÊPES

Makes 10 crêpes

1 cup (125g) all-purpose (plain) flour

1 ½ cups (375ml) milk

1 egg

2 Tbsp (30g) butter

Filling

5 Tbsp (75g) butter

3 ½ oz (100g) small white mushrooms, sliced

2 Tbsp all-purpose (plain) flour

1 ½ cups (375ml) milk

2 cups (60g) baby spinach leaves

14oz (410g) can sweetcorn kernels, drained

2 Tbsp snipped fresh chives

1 cup (125g) grated Swiss cheese

salt and freshly ground black pepper

arugula (rocket), for serving

Sift flour into a mixing bowl. Make a well in the center. Whisk milk and egg together, then gradually whisk into the flour until mixture is smooth (batter should be the consistency of pouring cream). Set aside for 15 minutes.

To make the filling, melt 1 tablespoon of butter in a large saucepan over medium heat and sauté the mushrooms until soft. Remove mushrooms to a bowl and set aside.

Wipe saucepan clean, then add remaining butter and melt over medium heat. Add flour and cook, stirring, for 1 minute. Remove from heat. Gradually add milk, whisking constantly, until combined and mixture is smooth. Return to heat and cook, stirring, for 3 to 5 minutes, until the sauce thickens and comes to a boil. Simmer for 3 minutes.

Stir in mushrooms, spinach, corn, chives and half the cheese. Season to taste with salt and pepper. Cover sauce and keep it warm.

Melt a knob of the butter in an 8 inch (20cm) non-stick crêpe pan. Add ¼ cup of batter, swirling to cover the base. Cook for 1 to 2 minutes, loosen and flip. Cook another minute. Repeat with remaining mixture.

Preheat broiler (grill) to high heat. Divide spinach and corn filling among crêpes. Fold into fourths or roll up. Arrange crêpes in an ovenproof dish. Sprinkle with the remaining cheese and broil (grill) for 1 to 2 minutes, until cheese bubbles. Serve with arugula.

GADO GADO SALAD

Serves 4

small head of cauliflower, cut in florets

9oz (250g) green beans, ends trimmed

1 large Yukon potato (or other waxy potato), peeled and diced

12oz (350g) firm tofu

3 Tbsp rice flour

½ cup (125ml) peanut oil

1 long cucumber, halved lengthwise and thinly sliced crosswise

1 large carrot, peeled and cut into matchsticks

1 cup (80g) mung bean sprouts

4 medium tomatoes, sliced

2 hard-boiled eggs, quartered

¼ cup (10g) chopped cilantro (coriander)

Satay sauce

1 Tbsp peanut oil

¼ onion, finely diced

1 clove garlic, crushed

½ habañero, deseeded and chopped

1 ½ tsp light brown (soft brown) sugar

1 Tbsp soy sauce

juice of ½ lemon

½ cup (75g) unsalted roasted peanuts

½ cup (125ml) water

Steam cauliflower, beans and potato until just tender. Set aside to cool.

Cut tofu into thick slices and pat dry on paper towels. Heat oil in a wok on high heat. Dredge tofu strips in flour, shake gently to remove any excess and fry quickly in hot oil, until golden. Drain on paper towels.

To make the satay sauce, heat oil in wok on a low heat, add onion and garlic and cook for 8 minutes, until onion is soft. Add the habañero, sugar, soy sauce and lemon juice and cook for 1 minute.

Add the peanuts and water to the pan and remove from heat. Purée the mixture, using a handheld blender, to form a thick sauce. Return sauce to the heat and simmer for 5 minutes, until reduced and thickened.

Arrange all the vegetables on serving plates. Top with fried tofu and the egg . Spoon satay sauce on top and garnish with cilantro.

PAPRIKA VEGETABLE POLENTA BAKE

Serves 6

2 cups (500ml) water

½ cup (85g) instant polenta

1 cup (30g) parsley leaves + extra for serving

¼ cup (25g) grated parmesan

Roasted vegetables

2lb 3oz (1kg) pumpkin, seeded, peeled, cubed

1 red onion, thinly sliced

2 tablespoons oil

2 teaspoons paprika

leaves from 4 sprigs lemon thyme

Topping

9oz (250g) cherry tomatoes, quartered

¼ cup (30g) pine nuts

4 eggs

½ cup (125ml) cream

1 tsp salt

freshly ground black pepper

6oz (150g) ricotta, crumbled

1 cup basil pesto, for serving (see page 14)

Preheat oven to 400°F (200°C). Lightly grease an 11 x 7 inch (28 x 18cm) rectangular pan.

In a medium saucepan, bring water to a boil. Gradually sprinkle in polenta, stirring constantly. Reduce heat to low and simmer for 5 to 10 minutes, until polenta thickens.

Stir parsley and cheese into polenta.
Spoon into prepared pan, smoothing top.
Cool, then refrigerate for 1 hour until firm.

Meanwhile, to roast vegetables, combine
pumpkin, onion, oil, paprika and thyme
in a large baking dish. Bake for 25 to
30 minutes, until vegetables are tender.

Reduce oven to 350°F (180°C).

Arrange roasted vegetables on polenta.
Scatter tomatoes and pine nuts over
vegetables. Whisk the eggs and cream
together, and season with salt and pepper.
Pour over vegetables and dot ricotta on top.

Bake for 30 to 35 minutes, until golden.
Serve with pesto.

SPICY VEGETABLE ROLL

Serves 4

¼ cup (55g) brown rice

1 Tbsp wild rice

2 zucchini (courgettes), halved lengthwise and sliced

2 medium-sized eggplants (aubergines), halved lengthwise and sliced

1 onion, cut into wedges

¼ cup (60ml) olive oil

salt and freshly ground black pepper

4½ oz (125g) canned chickpeas, rinsed and drained

½ cup (90g) sliced chargrilled bell pepper (capsicum)

1½ Tbsp readymade harissa paste (see glossary, page 309)

2 cups (60g) baby spinach

4oz (100g) haloumi, cut into small dice

⅓ cup (40g) pine nuts, toasted

16 sheets filo pastry, covered with a clean, damp dish towel

olive oil spray, for filo

2 eggs, lightly beaten

2 Tbsp readymade za'atar spice mix (see glossary, page 309)

Minted yogurt

2 Tbsp chopped mint

1 cup (225g) unsweetened natural yogurt

pinch of salt

Preheat oven to 400ºF (200ºC). Lightly grease and line a baking sheet with parchment paper.

Cook both types of rice together in a medium saucepan of boiling, salted water for 30 to 35 minutes, until tender. Drain and transfer rice to a large mixing bowl.

In another mixing bowl, toss the zucchini, eggplant and onion with oil and season with salt and pepper. Heat a large, non-stick skillet (fry-pan) on a high heat and sauté

zucchini and eggplant, in two batches, for 2 to 3 minutes each side, until just tender.

Put all the cooked vegetables back in the large skillet, and add chickpeas, chargrilled pepper and harissa paste. Stir to combine. Cook for 1 to 2 minutes over high heat, until fragrant. Add to rice in mixing bowl, along with spinach, cheese and pine nuts. Mix.

Working quickly, layer 4 sheets of filo pastry together, spraying top side of each with oil. Spoon one fourth of the vegetable

mixture along the longest edge of the pastry, leaving a 1 inch (2.5 cm) border. Brush pastry edges with egg, folding sides in.

Roll pastry tightly from the long side, to form a long log. Coil the length of filo into a snail shape and place on prepared sheet. Secure coil with toothpicks, if necessary. Brush filo generously with egg and sprinkle with 2 teaspoons of za'atar. Repeat layering, filling and rolling with remaining filo, adding to the coil, or making 4 individual coils.

Bake the coil or coils for 10 to 15 minutes, until golden and crisp.

Meanwhile, to make minted yogurt, stir the ingredients together. Serve spicy vegetable roll with the minted yogurt.

STIR-FRIED TOFU & BROCCOLINI

Serves 4

11oz (300g) firm tofu, patted dry and sliced into 12 even pieces

flour, for dusting

3 Tbsp vegetable oil

1 red bell pepper (capsicum), deseeded and thinly sliced

1 red onion, thinly sliced

1 tsp finely grated ginger

1 clove garlic, crushed

9oz (250g) broccolini

9oz (250g) baby pak choy, sliced into 4, lengthwise

4oz (100g) snap peas, ends trimmed

¼ cup (60ml) vegetable stock or water

3 Tbsp soy sauce

1 Tbsp Thai sweet chili sauce

1 tsp sesame oil

cooked rice noodles, for serving

Coat tofu with flour, shaking off any excess.

Heat oil in a wok or large fry-pan on high. Fry tofu in batches for 3 to 5 minutes, until crisp and golden. Drain on paper towels.

Add pepper, onion, ginger and garlic to wok and stir-fry for 1 minute. Add broccolini, pak choy and snap peas and stir-fry for 2 minutes.

Add stock or water, soy sauce, sweet chili sauce and sesame oil and stir-fry for a further 1 minute.

Return tofu to wok and gently toss to combine. Serve with rice noodles.

VEGETABLE TAGINE

Serves 4

4 tsp olive oil

1 red onion, sliced

4 tsp ras el hanout (see glossary, page 309)

1 inch (2.5cm) piece fresh ginger, grated

1 clove garlic, crushed

1 cinnamon stick

2 x 14oz (410g) cans chopped tomatoes

2 cups (500ml) vegetable stock

14oz (400g) sweet potato, peeled, cut into 1 inch (2.5cm) chunks

1 small eggplant (aubergine), diced

1 zucchini (courgette), halved lengthwise and chopped

1 carrot, halved, sliced crosswise

1 cup (100g) cauliflower florets

14oz (410g) can chickpeas, rinsed and drained

4oz (100g) green beans, trimmed and halved crosswise

salt

¼ cup (10g) roughly chopped parsley

prepared couscous, for serving

Heat the olive oil in a large saucepan on medium heat. Sauté onion for 3 minutes, until soft.

Add ras el hanout, ginger, garlic and cinnamon stick. Cook for 1 to 2 minutes, until aromatic. Stir in tomatoes and stock and add sweet potato.

Bring to the boil, then reduce heat and simmer, covered, for 8 minutes. Add eggplant, zucchini, carrot and cauliflower and cook for a further 10 minutes.

Mix in the chickpeas and beans and season to taste with salt. Cook for 2 minutes more.

Stir parsley through just before serving. Serve with couscous.

BAKED MUSHROOM CRÊPES

Serves 6

1 cup (125g) whole wheat (wholemeal) flour

1 cup (125g) all-purpose (plain) flour

1 cup (250ml) cold water

1 cup (250ml) milk

4 eggs

4 Tbsp (60g) butter, melted

3 cups (750ml) tomato passata from a jar

1 cup (125g) grated mozzarella

Filling

2 Tbsp vegetable oil

2 Tbsp butter

1 onion, chopped

1 clove garlic, crushed

6 large portabella mushrooms, sliced

4oz (120g) baby spinach leaves

salt and freshly ground black pepper

9oz (250g) ricotta

4oz (100g) feta, crumbled

1 tsp pumpkin pie spice (mixed spice)

Whisk flours in a large mixing bowl. Whisk together water, milk and eggs in a separate bowl. Gradually add to flour, whisking until batter is smooth. Stir butter into batter. Set aside, covered, for 20 minutes.

To make the filling, heat oil and butter in a large skillet (fry-pan) on medium heat. Sauté onion and garlic for 1 to 2 minutes, until onion is soft. Add mushrooms and cook, stirring, for 3 to 4 minutes, until tender. Stir in spinach and cook until wilted. Season to taste with salt and pepper, then set aside to cool.

In a small bowl, combine ricotta, feta and pumpkin pie spice. Season to taste.

Preheat oven to 350ºF (180ºC). Grease an ovenproof dish.

Brush the base of a 7 ½ inch (19 cm) non-stick skillet with oil. Heat on high.

Add ¼ cup (60ml) ladles of batter to the hot pan, swirling to cover base — quickly pour out any excess. Cook crêpes for 1 to 2 minutes, until lightly golden. Turn and cook the other side for 30 seconds. Transfer to a plate. Repeat with remaining batter.

Spoon a layer of ricotta mixture and a layer of mushroom mixture onto each crêpe. Roll up and arrange crêpes in a single layer in prepared dish.

Pour passata over crêpes and sprinkle with mozzarella. Bake for 10 to 15 minutes, until hot and golden.

VEGETABLE BIRYANI

Serves 4

2 Tbsp vegetable oil

1 eggplant (aubergine), cut into ½ inch
(1.2 cm) cubes

2 cups (200g) cauliflower florets

1 large onion, thinly sliced

3 cloves garlic, crushed

2 tsp finely grated ginger

2 long green chilies, thinly sliced

4 tsp garam masala (see glossary,
page 307)

4 whole cloves

3 tsp turmeric

1 ½ cups (330g) basmati rice, rinsed

3 cups (750ml) vegetable stock

½ cup (75g) frozen peas

½ cup (80g) currants

4 Tbsp cilantro (coriander) leaves,
for serving

½ cup (110g) unsweetened natural yogurt,
for serving

Heat half the oil in a large saucepan on high heat. Sauté eggplant and cauliflower for 3 to 4 minutes, until golden. Transfer to a plate.

Heat remaining oil in same pan. Sauté onion for 6 to 8 minutes, until golden. Add garlic, ginger, chili and spices. Cook for 1 minute, until aromatic.

Add rice, stirring to coat well with spice mixture. Add stock and bring to a boil on high heat, then reduce heat to very low and simmer, covered, for 8 minutes.

Add eggplant mixture, peas and currants to rice. Cook, covered, for a further 3 to 5 minutes, until vegetables are tender. Remove from heat and set aside for 5 minutes. Scatter cilantro over biryani and serve with yogurt.

POTATO-TOPPED VEGETABLE PIE

Serves 6

3 large Desiree potatoes (or other all-purpose potatoes), peeled

1 Tbsp vegetable oil

1 leek, trimmed and sliced

2 cloves garlic, crushed

1 cauliflower, cut into florets

2 carrots, peeled and diced

2 x 14oz (410g) cans diced tomatoes

2 x 14oz (410g) cans lentils, rinsed and drained

1 cup (150g) frozen peas

salt and freshly ground black pepper

¼ cup (25g) grated parmesan

Preheat oven to 400°F (200°C).

Steam potatoes for 8 minutes over boiling water, until just starting to become tender. Remove from heat; cool.

Heat oil in a large saucepan on medium heat. Cook leek and garlic for 3 to 4 minutes, until soft. Add cauliflower and carrot and cook for 5 minutes, until beginning to soften.

Add tomato and lentils. Bring to a boil, reduce heat to low and simmer for 10 minutes, until vegetables are tender.

Add peas and season to taste with salt and pepper. Spoon into an 8 cup (2 litre) capacity ovenproof dish.

Coarsely grate potato and combine with parmesan. Season well. Pile onto vegetables. Bake 30 minutes, until golden and bubbling. Serve immediately.

WINTER VEGETABLE STEW WITH CARAWAY DUMPLINGS

Serves 4-6

1 Tbsp olive oil

2 leeks, trimmed and thinly sliced

2 rutabagas (swedes) or 4 parsnips, peeled and roughly chopped

2 celery ribs, roughly chopped

2 carrots, peeled and roughly chopped

1 onion, roughly chopped

2 cups (500ml) vegetable stock

14oz (410g) can cannellini beans, rinsed and drained

14oz (410g) can diced tomatoes

1 Tbsp tomato paste

1 Tbsp soy sauce

1 bay leaf

4 Tbsp fresh oregano leaves, for serving

Caraway dumplings

2 ½ cups (150g) soft fresh breadcrumbs

2 eggs, lightly beaten

1 tsp caraway seeds

finely grated zest of 1 lemon

½ tsp salt

Preheat oven to 350°F (180°C).

Heat oil in a large saucepan on medium-high heat. Sauté leek, rutabaga, celery, carrot and onion for 4 to 5 minutes, until onion is soft.

Add stock, cannellini beans, tomatoes, tomato paste, soy sauce and bay leaf. Bring mixture to a boil, then transfer to a large casserole dish.

Bake, covered, for 20 minutes. Uncover and bake a further 10 minutes.

Meanwhile, to make caraway dumplings, combine all the ingredients in a mixing bowl. Using wet hands, shape tablespoons of the mixture into balls.

Arrange dumplings on top of stew, pushing them down slightly into the vegetables. Bake stew, covered, for 5 to 10 minutes, or until the dumplings soften. Serve, sprinkled with oregano leaves.

SPICY CHICKPEA & CARAMELIZED ONION COUSCOUS

Serves 4

1 cup (180g) instant couscous

1 tsp ground turmeric

1 cup (250ml) vegetable stock

3 Tbsp olive oil

3 large onions, finely sliced

14oz (410g) can chickpeas, rinsed and drained

3 Tbsp chopped cilantro (coriander)

salt and freshly ground black pepper

Place couscous in a bowl and stir in turmeric. Bring stock to a boil and immediately pour over couscous. Stir briefly to combine, then cover with plastic wrap and set aside to steam for 10 minutes.

Meanwhile, heat oil in a skillet (fry-pan) on medium heat. Add onion and cook for 10 minutes until golden brown and caramelized. Add chickpeas and cook for a few minutes more, to heat through.

Fluff up couscous with a fork. Stir in the caramelized onion and chickpeas. Season with salt and pepper, to taste, and serve with cilantro scattered on top.

SOFT POLENTA WITH MEDITERRANEAN VEGETABLES

Serves 4

1 small eggplant (aubergine), cut into thin wedges

2 zucchini, cut into batons

2 tomatoes, cut into wedges

1 red bell pepper (capsicum), halved lengthwise, deseeded and cut into wide strips

1 onion, cut into wedges

2 cloves garlic, sliced

3 Tbsp (10g) thyme sprigs

4 tsp olive oil

1 tsp salt

freshly ground black pepper

1 cup (170g) instant polenta

½ cup (40g) grated parmesan + shaved parmesan, to serve

Preheat oven to 425°F (220°C).

Combine eggplant, zucchini, tomato, pepper, onion, garlic, thyme and olive oil in a roasting pan with salt and pepper. Toss well to coat. Roast for 40 minutes, stirring once or twice, until vegetables are tender.

Meanwhile, bring 2½ cups (625ml) water to a boil in a large heavy-based saucepan on high heat. Pour in polenta, stirring constantly until boiling. Reduce heat to low and cook for 5 minutes, stirring. Remove from heat, stir in the grated parmesan, cover and keep warm for up to 5 minutes.

Spoon polenta into bowls and top with roasted vegetables. Serve with shaved parmesan over the top.

SIDE
DISHES

SUPREME SALADS

A great salad can be the best dish of your day, be it a simple collection of leafy greens to accompany a heartier dish or a collection of more substantial ingredients that makes an entire meal.

Use only the best seasonal produce: delight in the joys of asparagus, fennel and artichokes in spring, enjoy the warmth of summer tomatoes, peppers and cucumbers, pile on carrots, squash, nuts and greens in the cooler months.

Add protein to transform salads into more substantial meals. Cheese spices up a salad with both protein and flavor. Try a classic Greek salad with feta, tomatoes, cucumber and olives or add parmesan shavings to arugula (rocket) and pear for a tasty snack. Tofu and tempeh work well with Asian flavors, try marinating them first for extra flavor. Hardboiled eggs are a quick and easy protein fix; they can take many flavors and textures from mayonnaise to curry powder; celery to pine nuts, and they work well in potato salads. Nuts are a wonderful way to add extra flavor and texture to most salads.

Experiment with grains and pulses to transform the everyday into something exotic. Quinoa or chickpeas added to your favorite roasted vegetables make a nutritious meal. Lentils and rice are a great base for a variety of flavors.

The right salad dressing is vital. Homemade is always best; use the best oil and vinegar you can afford, and ensure you have a balance of sweet, salty and sharp flavors. Salad greens should be washed and dried well. If there is too much water, your dressing will not coat the leaves. Don't over do it: remember, salad dressing serves to accentuate the flavors of the ingredients, not drown them.

Fresh herbs can make all the difference. Aside from classic combinations such as basil and tomato, most salads benefit from the addition of fresh herbs. Think fresh crunchy mint, cilantro (coriander), parsley, chives and dill. Keep a living herb pot in your garden for a constant supply.

ENTERTAINING MENU
A MEDITERRANEAN GRILL

There's no better place for summer entertaining than the great outdoors, be it at the beach, a secret picnic spot, or in your own backyard. Vegetarians don't have to miss out on the barbecue season. Be inspired by the sun-kissed flavors of Mediterranean cuisines with this complete menu, suitable for summer entertaining.

If you are cooking for both vegetarians and meat lovers, you could choose just a couple of these recipes as part of a larger menu, to make sure that your vegetarian guests are catered for. Don't forget plenty of chilled drinks and a big basket of fresh bread to complete the table.

Appetizers
- White bean dip with grilled vegetables
- Bell pepper and haloumi parcels

Entrée and side dishes
- Grilled spinach cheese parcels
- Grilled asparagus with arugula and parmesan
- Tomato and basil salad
- Piquant cucumber and radish salad

For dessert, select the best ripe fruit of the season and serve with a selection of scooped sorbets or gelati from your favorite store.

GRILLED ASPARAGUS WITH ARUGULA & PARMESAN

Serves 4

1 bunch fresh asparagus, trimmed

2 cloves garlic, crushed

3 Tbsp olive oil

salt and freshly ground black pepper

2 cups (60g) arugula (rocket)

½ cup (45g) shaved parmesan

1 Tbsp balsamic vinegar

Preheat a chargrill pan to medium-hot.

Place the asparagus in a bowl with the garlic, add the oil and toss well. Season with salt and pepper and chargrill for 1 to 3 minutes on each side, turning once during cooking, until tender.

Serve asparagus scattered with arugula and parmesan, and sprinkled with balsamic vinegar.

TOMATO & BASIL SALAD

Serves 4

4 large ripe tomatoes, thinly sliced

1 shallot, finely chopped

8 basil leaves, roughly torn

3 Tbsp extra virgin olive oil

1 Tbsp balsamic or wine vinegar

salt and freshly ground black pepper

Overlap tomato slices on a serving platter. Sprinkle with shallot and basil.

Spoon oil and vinegar evenly over salad. Season generously with salt and pepper.

Cook's note   Store tomatoes at room temperature. Refrigeration diminishes their flavor.

CAPONATA

Serves 4

2 Tbsp olive oil

1 large eggplant
(aubergine), diced

1 red bell pepper
(capsicum), deseeded and
cut into large dice

1 onion, finely chopped

14oz (410g) can diced
tomatoes

1 Tbsp drained capers

¼ cup (40g) pitted, halved
green olives

4 tsp sugar

3 Tbsp red wine vinegar

salt

Heat oil in a large skillet (fry-pan) on medium-high heat.
Sauté eggplant for 5 to 10 minutes, until browned and tender.
Set aside.

Add pepper and sauté until soft. Return eggplant to the pan
with onion and tomato and simmer for 15 minutes.

Stir in capers, olives, sugar and vinegar. Season with salt, to
taste. Simmer gently for another 20 minutes. Serve caponata
at room temperature.

GRILLED VEGETABLE SALAD

Serves 6

6 Japanese long eggplants (aubergines), trimmed

4 large zucchini (courgettes), trimmed

1 red bell pepper (capsicum), deseeded and thickly sliced

1 yellow bell pepper (capsicum), deseeded and thickly sliced

⅓ cup (80ml) olive oil

salt and freshly ground black pepper

3 Tbsp balsamic vinegar

Preheat a chargrill to medium.

Thickly slice eggplants and zucchini lengthwise. Place in a large bowl with sliced peppers and add olive oil. Season vegetables with salt and pepper and toss well to coat.

Chargrill the vegetables in batches for 2 to 3 minutes on each side, to brown. Remove to a bowl and cool slightly.

Sprinkle vegetables with balsamic vinegar and toss well to combine. Serve on a platter.

GRILLED MUSHROOMS

Serves 4

8 portabella mushrooms, stalks trimmed

½ cup (125ml) olive oil

2 cloves garlic, crushed

1 habañero, chopped

¼ cup (10g) chopped parsley, for serving

Preheat broiler (grill) to medium heat.

Lay mushrooms, stalk-side up, in a foil-lined pan.

Combine oil, garlic and habañero in a small bowl. Pour evenly over mushrooms.

Broil (grill) for 10 to 15 minutes, until tender and juicy. Serve sprinkled with parsley.

FENNEL, PEAR & PARMESAN SALAD

Serves 4

1 large fennel bulb, thinly
sliced

1 firm sweet pear, unpeeled,
sliced

4 tsp fresh lemon juice

4 tsp extra virgin olive oil

sea salt and freshly ground
black pepper

¼ cup (25g) shaved
parmesan

Arrange fennel and pear slices in a shallow serving bowl.
Add lemon juice and toss immediately to coat well. (The lemon
juice prevents the fennel and pear from darkening.)

Just before serving, add oil and plenty of salt and pepper.
Toss again.

Scatter parmesan over salad.

CRUNCHY PEANUT BUTTER NOODLES

Serves 4

7oz (200g) dried egg noodles

1 Tbsp sesame oil

¾ cup (225g) crunchy peanut butter

1 Tbsp finely grated fresh ginger

3 Tbsp dark soy sauce

2 Tbsp warm water

½ cup (75g) roasted unsalted peanuts

Cook noodles in boiling water for 3 to 4 minutes, until just tender to the bite. Drain well and toss with sesame oil to stop noodles sticking together.

Blend peanut butter, ginger, soy sauce and water together to make a creamy dressing.

Mix noodles with peanut butter dressing. Serve scattered with roasted peanuts.

GRILLED ZUCCHINI SALAD WITH MINT

Serves 4

2lb 3oz (1kg) zucchini (courgettes), sliced lengthwise

3 Tbsp extra virgin olive oil

2 cloves garlic, thinly sliced

1 cup (30g) mint leaves

4 tsp white wine vinegar

sea salt and freshly ground black pepper

Preheat a large chargrill or ridged pan on medium heat.

Brush zucchini with olive oil and cook in batches for 2 to 3 minutes each side, until tender and showing grill marks. Arrange on a serving platter.

Scatter garlic over zucchini, then add mint. Spoon vinegar evenly over the zucchini, season with salt and pepper and toss gently to combine.

Stand salad at room temperature to marinate for at least 1 hour before serving.

LENTIL, CORN & TOMATO SALAD

Serves 4

1 cup (200g) puy lentils

2 large cloves garlic, crushed with flat side of a knife

salt

2 sweetcorn cobs, husks and silk removed

9oz (250g) cherry tomatoes, halved

4 scallions (spring onions), thinly sliced

¼ cup (10g) chopped dill

¼ cup (10g) torn basil leaves

3 Tbsp red wine vinegar

¼ cup (60ml) extra virgin olive oil

Combine lentils, garlic and ½ teaspoon salt in a saucepan. Add enough water to cover lentils. Cover and bring to a boil. Reduce heat and simmer for 20 minutes, until lentils are tender. Drain and transfer to a large bowl.

Meanwhile, cook sweetcorn in a saucepan of boiling, salted water for 4 minutes. Drain. Using a sharp knife, cut kernels from cobs. Combine with lentils.

Add remaining ingredients to lentil mixture and season to taste. Toss well to combine and season with salt, to taste. Serve warm.

SESAME GREENS & OYSTER MUSHROOMS

Serves 4

1 Tbsp vegetable oil

2 cloves garlic, sliced

2 long red chilies, sliced

9oz (250g) Chinese broccoli (gai lan), roughly chopped

4oz (120g) green beans, trimmed and halved

4oz (120g) snap peas

10 oyster mushrooms, sliced

6 scallions (spring onions), sliced

1 bunch broccolini, roughly chopped

¼ cup (60ml) kecap manis (see glossary, page 310)

3 Tbsp water

1 Tbsp light soy sauce

toasted sesame seeds, for serving

Heat oil in a wok on high heat. Stir-fry garlic and chili for 30 seconds.

Add all vegetables. Stir-fry for 3 minutes, until just softened.

Add kecap manis, water and soy sauce. Stir-fry for another 3 to 4 minutes.

Serve sprinkled with sesame seeds.

GARDEN SALAD WITH WALNUTS

Serves 6

3 Tbsp white wine vinegar

2 tsp Dijon mustard

½ tsp sugar

1 clove garlic, crushed

⅓ cup (80ml) extra virgin olive oil

salt and freshly ground black pepper

9oz (250g) baby cos leaves

4oz (100g) arugula (rocket)

⅓ cup (40g) roughly chopped walnuts

Place vinegar, mustard, sugar and garlic in a small bowl. Whisk until combined. Gradually add oil, whisking, until dressing thickens slightly. Season to taste with salt and pepper. Set aside.

Arrange salad leaves in a bowl, sprinkle with walnuts and pour dressing over the top. Toss lightly to combine.

ASPARAGUS WITH CAPER AND EGG SAUCE

Serves 6

1 hard-boiled egg, peeled and chopped

1 Tbsp chopped parsley

1 Tbsp baby capers

1 Tbsp finely chopped cornichons (pickled baby cucumbers)

3 bunches asparagus, trimmed

⅓ cup (80ml) extra virgin olive oil

3 Tbsp red wine vinegar

2 tsp Dijon mustard

salt and freshly ground black pepper

Combine egg, parsley, capers and cornichons in a small bowl.

Cook asparagus in a large saucepan of boiling, salted water for 2 minutes, until just tender. Drain and keep warm.

Meanwhile, combine oil, vinegar and mustard in a small saucepan. Heat on medium for 1 to 2 minutes, until warm. Pour over egg mixture and season with salt and pepper.

Spoon the sauce over the asparagus and serve warm or at room temperature.

PIQUANT CUCUMBER & RADISH SALAD

Serves 4

1 long cucumber, thinly sliced

½ tsp salt

1lb (450g) radishes, trimmed and thinly sliced

3 Tbsp white wine vinegar

3 Tbsp snipped dill

Place cucumber in a colander and sprinkle with salt. Toss gently. Stand for 5 minutes. Press cucumber lightly to drain excess liquid.

Place radish and cucumber in a serving bowl. Add vinegar and dill; toss to combine.

BEANS, LEEKS & ALMONDS

Serves 6

7oz (200g) yellow beans, trimmed

7oz (200g) green beans, trimmed

2 cups (300g) frozen double-peeled fava (broad) beans

7oz (200g) snow peas (mangetouts), trimmed

1 Tbsp olive oil

1 small leek, washed, trimmed and thinly sliced

2 cloves garlic, sliced

2 Tbsp slivered almonds

Blanch all beans with snow peas in a large saucepan of boiling, salted water. Drain, plunge into iced water and drain again. Slice snow peas diagonally.

Heat oil in a skillet (fry-pan) on high heat. Sauté leek, garlic and almonds for 3 minutes, until leek is soft.

Add beans and snow peas and cook gently for another 1 to 2 minutes, until heated through.

BROWN RICE & AVOCADO SALAD

Serves 6

1 cup (220g) brown rice

1 avocado, diced

9oz (250g) cherry tomatoes, halved

juice of 3 limes

½ cup (15g) chopped cilantro (coriander)

salt and freshly ground black pepper

Cook brown rice in plenty of boiling water for 30 minutes, until just tender to the bite. Drain well and set aside for 30 minutes to cool completely.

Combine cold rice with other ingredients in a salad bowl. Season with salt and pepper and toss to combine.

ROASTED CHILI GARLIC EGGPLANT

Serves 6

⅓ cup (80ml) olive oil

3 medium eggplants (aubergines), thinly sliced crosswise

2 cloves garlic, thinly sliced

½ tsp dried chili flakes

1 tsp salt

freshly ground black pepper

¼ cup (10g) chopped parsley

¼ cup (10g) chopped mint

juice and finely grated zest of 1 lemon

Preheat oven to 400°F (200°C).

Heat 1 tablespoon oil in large skillet (fry-pan) on medium heat. Cook eggplant in batches for 2 to 3 minutes each side, until lightly browned, Transfer to a large ovenproof dish. Sprinkle with garlic and chili. Season with salt and pepper.

Bake for 20 to 25 minutes, until eggplant is tender.

Meanwhile, combine parsley, mint, lemon juice and zest in a small bowl.

Serve eggplant sprinkled with lemon herb mixture.

HOT POTATO SALAD

Serves 6

2lb 3oz (1kg) small boiling
potatoes, larger ones cut
in half

⅓ cup (80g) sour cream

4 dill pickles (gherkins),
finely diced

4 Tbsp chopped mint leaves

2 Tbsp chopped dill

salt and freshly ground
black pepper

Cook potatoes in plenty of boiling, salted water for 12 minutes,
or until tender. Drain well. Place potatoes in a serving bowl.

Meanwhile, combine sour cream, dill pickles, mint and dill in
a bowl and season with salt and pepper to make a dressing.

Pour dressing over potatoes while still hot, toss well and
serve immediately.

GLOSSARY

Proteins

The protein component of a vegetarian diet comes from many varied sources. These include eggs, dairy foods (milk, cream, cheese, yogurt), soy products (soy milk, tofu, tempeh, seitan), nuts, seeds, pulses (lentils, beans and peas) and grains (rice, wheat, oats).

About soy products

- Soy milk is made from ground soy beans.
- Tofu is made from coagulated soy milk.
- Silken tofu is soft. It is well-suited to steaming, for adding to soups and for blending into spreads and dips.
- Firm tofu is suitable for shallow or deep-frying, which gives it a crispy golden coating, and for stir-frying.
- Tempeh is made from pressed whole soy beans. It can be used in similar ways to firm tofu.
- Seitan or Textured Vegetable Protein is a soy-based product formed to imitate meat, and comes in various forms.

Miso paste

- Made from fermented soy beans, grain, salt and water, miso paste is very rich in flavor, making it an ideal flavor base for soups and stews. It can also be blended with other ingredients and used as a marinade.

Rice

- **Arborio** This Italian variety of rice releases a lot of starch as it is cooked, making it ideal for risotto. It creates its own creamy sauce as it cooks. For best results, stir risotto constantly while cooking.
- **Jasmine** This long-grained rice is fluffy and delicately fragrant. Often used in Thai cookery, it is also suitable as a general cooking rice.
- **Basmati** This Indian variety of long-grain rice is firm and nuttily fragrant. Used for biryani and served with curry, it can also be used as a general cooking rice.
- **Long-grain and short-grain white rice** These varieties are widely grown as general cooking rices. Short-grain rice is firm and

glossy and is perfect for sushi or a side dish. Long-grain rice is fluffier than short.

- **Brown rice** This rice has had the outer husk removed, but not the next layer of bran and germ (white rice has had all of these removed). Brown rice contains more nutrients than white. It is very flavorsome and can be used in many recipes, such as pilafs, stir-fries and salads.

- **Wild rice** Technically a grass seed, and not a rice, there are four varieties of wild rice; three are native to North America and one variety to China. Wild rice has a wonderful purple color, is high in protein, and tastes quite nutty. It can be used alone or mixed with other rices.

Polenta

- Also known as cornmeal, polenta is ground yellow or white maize, and comes in various sizes, from fine to coarse. It is also available as instant (quick-cook) or traditional (slow-cook) polenta. When it is cooked with water, polenta becomes soft and mushy, and is very starchy. It can be served soft, or it can be allowed to cool and become firm. It can then be baked, grilled or fried. It can also be formed into fritters or dumplings or used as a flour.

- In the USA, grits are similar to coarse polenta, but the maize for grits is either par-boiled or treated with lye.

Quinoa

- (pronounced KEEN-wah) is a South American grain that is high in protein, gluten-free and quick to cook.

Pearl barley

- Barley grains that have been hulled, had the bran removed and then been through a polishing process are called pearl barley. It is used in soups and stews, versions of risotto, and is also processed into flour and flakes.

Pasta

- There are many shapes of pasta; Italian cooks match the shape of pasta to the type of sauce. Cup shapes, short tubes, and those with ridges are used with chunky sauces, while long and smooth noodles are matched

with smoother sauces. Sheets of pasta are used for rolling or layering, or for forming into parcels such as ravioli.
- Fresh pasta can be cooked very quickly in plenty of boiling, well-salted water.
- Dried pasta takes much longer to cook, also in plenty of boiling, well-salted water. Check packet for cooking time.
- As to quantity, the rule of thumb is 2oz (55g) of dry pasta per person for a first course or side dish, and 3 to 4oz (85 to 115 g) per person for a main course.

Mushroom varieties
- **Small white (button)** Young white mushrooms are rounded in shape, mild in flavor and moderately firm. They can be used whole or sliced in most recipes.
- **Brown** Young brown mushrooms are extremely similar to white, except in color.
- **Portabella (brown crimini or flatcap)** Large white or brown mushrooms eventually thicken and flatten out in the cap area, and are then known as portabella mushrooms. Use them in sautés and stews, or broil (grill) them.

- **Enokitake (enoki)** These fine, needle-like mushrooms are very delicate, and should only be added to a dish just before serving.
- **Shiitake** Very firm, flavorsome mushrooms. Remove stalks before use. Dried shiitake can be reconstituted in hot water and then used in the same ways as fresh ones.

Cooking oils
- Match the oil you use to the dish:
- Light vegetable oils are good for general frying and stir-frying.
- Peanut oil is good for frying food with crispy coatings, as well as for many Asian dishes.
- Heavier, tasty oils such as olive or grapeseed oil are ideal for Mediterranean cookery.
- Sesame oil is very strong and should only be used sparingly as a flavoring, rather than used as a cooking oil.

Salad oils

- The oil you use in a salad dressing is a vital ingredient in the salad, so choose it to match the other components.
- Extra virgin olive oil is very flavorsome, and only needs citrus juice or vinegar, and salt, to become a delicious dressing.
- Lighter vegetable or salad oils are ideal for making mayonnaise, and are useful in vinaigrette dressings that have other strong ingredients, such as mustard or garlic.
- Nut oils such as almond or walnut oil are great for salads. They are quite strong in flavor so can be used in conjunction with a light vegetable oil.
- Avocado oil is harder to find but makes a delicious alternative to olive oil.

Tahini

This rich paste is made from sesame seeds. It is used to flavor hummus, Middle Eastern dressings and marinades. It is also the main ingredient in some types of halva, a Middle Eastern sweet.

Tamari

This is a type of Japanese soy sauce, originally made using the by-product of miso roduction. Some tamari contains no wheat, so is useful for people with gluten intolerance.

Mirin

A Japanese rice wine, is used for cookery, rather than for drinking.

Palm sugar

Mainly produced in South-East Asia from the sap of various palm trees, it is sold in solid blocks which can be grated, or as a thick paste. Golden brown in color, it has a light caramel flavor. It is used frequently in Thai cookery. Light brown (soft brown) sugar can be used as a substitute.

Tamarind

A sour paste from the bean pods of the tamarind tree. It is commonly used in Asian, African and Caribbean cookery and is sold in various forms:

- **Tamarind pulp** is sold in blocks which need to be soaked in water, gently mixed into the water and then sieved to give a brown tamarind liquid.
- **Tamarind purée** is sieved pulp blended with a little water.
- **Tamarind water** is sieved pulp blended with plenty of water.

Kaffir lime leaves (makrut)

The leaves of the Asian kaffir lime tree are very fragrant, and are used to flavor many Thai dishes as well as food from other South-East Asian countries. Whole leaves are used to impart flavor to curries and soups (the whole leaves are not eaten), and finely shredded leaves are added to salads and stir-fries (the shredded leaves can be eaten). Key lime or Tahitian lime leaves can be used whole to add a similar flavor to dishes (these are not eaten).

Spice mixes

- **Garam masala** is a dry Indian spice blend; it has no one recipe — it is blended to suit the cook, their region, and the dish they are making. Common ingredients include several peppers, cloves, cardamom, nutmeg, cumin and star anise, but many other spices may also be included. Garam masala is added to many dishes as a seasoning or spice base.
- **Piri piri seasoning** Piri piri are pungent, small red chilis. Piri piri seasoning is Portuguese; it contains crushed chilies, itrus peel, onion, garlic, pepper, salt, lemon juice, bay leaves, paprika, pimiento, basil, oregano, and tarragon.
- **Za'atar** A Middle Eastern and North African seasoning blend, typically made from a

mixture of dried sumac, sesame seeds and thyme. Sometimes other ingredients such as salt, oregano, cumin seeds and savory are added. Used as a seasoning, it is also delicious served with bread and olive oil.

- **Ras el hanout** A dry Moroccan spice blend, and as with garam masala the recipe varies. It contains a large number of spices and is added to many dishes as a seasoning or spice base.

- **Harissa paste** This fiery Moroccan paste is a blend of chilies, salt, olive oil and spices; usually coriander, cumin and caraway seeds. Some commercial harissa pastes have a milder flavor through the addition of roasted peppers (capiscum) or tomato paste. It is traditionally used as a condiment, alongside the cooling agent, yogurt.

- **Thai curry pastes** The most common Thai curry pastes are red curry paste, green, Penang and Mussaman. Each one is a finely blended mixture of dry and fresh spices, vegetables and herbs; some contain hot chili and others are sweet and mild. Two other common ingredients in Thai curry pastes are dried prawn paste (belachan), and fish sauce. Vegetarian versions are available, so always check the ingredients list. Recipes are also easy to find. When making vegetarian versions of these pastes, use the substitutes suggested below.

Avoiding non-vegetarian ingredients in Asian recipes

Many Asian vegetable-based recipes contain non-vegetarian ingredients. Here are some useful substitutions that you can make:

- Replace oyster sauce with kecap manis, which is a thick sweet soy sauce, or hoisin sauce, which is also thick and sweet
- Replace fish sauce with light soy sauce
- Replace prawn paste (belachan) with a little dark soy sauce or kecap manis
- Fish, chicken or meat stock can be replaced with vegetable stock, and often with water.

Making and storing vegetable stock

- Vegetable stock is easily made by gently simmering vegetables and herbs in plenty of water for 1 to 2 hours. Strain the vegetables and store the remaining stock in the refrigerator or freezer.

- While any combination can be used, the base ingredients are usually carrot, onion, celery, peppercorns, parsley stems and bay leaf. Mushrooms give good body to a vegetable stock; Very starchy root vegetables are usually not used. Herbs can be varied to suit the requirements.
- Stock can be refrigerated for several days, or frozen for several months.

Basic pizza dough

1 cup (250ml) warm water
½ tsp sugar
2 tsp active dry yeast
2 cups (250g) bread (strong) flour
1 tsp salt
1 Tbsp olive oil

Mix water, sugar and yeast in a small bowl and set aside to activate for 5 to 10 minutes, until mixture is foamy.

Place flour and salt in the bowl of an electric mixer, fitted with a dough hook. Add the foamy yeast mixture and the oil. Mix slowly until the mixture forms a ball of soft dough. If necessary, add a little more water to reach a smooth consistency. Continue to knead the pizza dough for 5 to 7 minutes, until it is glossy and elastic.

Place dough in a large, lightly oiled bowl, turning dough once so the whole ball of dough is oiled. Cover with plastic wrap and leave in a warm place to rise for approximately an hour, or until dough has doubled in volume.

Preheat oven to 400°F (200°C).

Knead the dough on a lightly floured surface for 1 minute and form into a ball. Roll out as thinly as possible. Top with chosen ingredients. Cook on a baking sheet or pizza stone until dough is crisp.

INDEX

ACKNOWLEDGMENTS

Recipes and images on pages 22-25, 30-33, 62-65, 72-73, 76-77, 80-81, 84-85, 94-97, 106-107, 114-115, 120-123, 128-131, 154-155, 158-159, 168-169, 172-175, 180-181, 200-201, 212-213, 216-217, 232-233, 238-239, 256-257, 266-267, 272-273, 278-279, 294-295 and 298-299 copyright *New Zealand Woman's Weekly*

Images on pages inside cover flap, 198, 302, 305, 308, 311, 314, 316, 319 and 320 copyright Shutterstock.com

All other recipes and images copyright acpsyndication.com